West Kent Co...

This book is due for return on o...
stamped below unless an extensi...

Psychology in Practice: Crime

PSYCHOLOGY
in Practice

Crime

Julie Harrower

Series Editor: Hugh Coolican

Hodder & Stoughton
A MEMBER OF THE HODDER HEADLINE GROUP

Orders: please contact Bookpoint Ltd, 130 Milton Park, Abingdon, Oxon OX14 4SB.
Telephone: (44) 01235 827720. Fax: (44) 01235 400454. Lines are open from 9.00 - 6.00,
Monday to Saturday, with a 24 hour message answering service.
Email address: orders@bookpoint.co.uk

British Library Cataloguing in Publication Data
A catalogue record for this title is available from the British Library

ISBN 0 340 84497 3

First Published 2001
Impression number   10 9 8 7 6 5 4 3 2 1
Year   2007 2006 2005 2004 2003 2002 2001

Typeset by Dorchester Typesetting Group Limited, Dorset, England
Printed in Great Britain for Hodder & Stoughton Educational, a division of Hodder Headline Plc,
338 Euston Road, London NW1 3BH by The Bath Press Ltd

ACKNOWLEDGEMENTS

The author and publisher would like to thank the following for permission to reproduce photographs: Figure 0.1 Peter Marshall/Photofusion, David Trainer/Photofusion; Figure 0.2 Professor Phillip Zimbardo; Figure 0.3 Bob Watkins/Photofusion; Figure 1.1 Popperfoto/Reuters; Figure 1.3 Paula Solloway/Format; Figure 2.1 PA Photos/EPA: Figure 3.2 Paul Doyle/Photofusion; Figure 4.1 PA News; Figure 4.2 Popperfoto/Reuters; Figure 5.1 Peter Jordan/PA Photos; Figure 5.2 Joanne O'Brien/Format; Figure 6.1 Fiona Hanson/PA News; Figure 6.2 London News Service; Figure 6.3 BFI Stills, Posters and Designs; Figure 7.1 Associated Press Photos/Sam Mircovich, Pool; Figure 7.2 BFI Stills, Posters and Designs; Figure 8.1 Jim Olive, Peter Arnold Inc/Science Photo Library; Figure 8.2 G. Montgomery/Photofusion.

CONTENTS

Introduction

We are all fascinated by crime, but only as long as we and our loved ones do not become victims. This paradox produces an ambivalent attitude to crime, and a real gulf between fiction and fact. We consume media representations of crime avidly, comforted to believe that there are unusually gifted individuals who draw uncannily accurate deductions about random events and in so doing solve crime, bringing perpetrators to justice. We also believe, because of the way these individuals are presented to us, that acute psychological insight can make a dramatic contribution to resolving the problem of crime. The reality is somewhat different, and unfortunately less comforting, but there certainly are ways in which psychology can make a valuable contribution to our understanding of crime.

The psychological analysis of criminal behaviour, and the application of psychological knowledge to offending patterns, rehabilitation strategies, and crime reduction can undoubtedly be a significant influence in our approach to crime. However, when members of the public think of the ways in which psychology has helped in the investigation of crime, they tend to focus on offender profiling because of media fascination with this technique and its application to violent, sexually related offences. The truth is that the history of psychology, its emphasis on individual differences, and its focus on systematic observation, rigorous methodology, and the collation of evidence, makes its potential as a contributor to the investigation of crime extremely valuable. Ironically, the current media presentation of offender profiling as one of the few successful areas of applied psychology probably makes it the least profitable avenue to explore if we are to fully understand how psychology is best applied to the study of crime.

In spite of some early links between research on perception and memory and evaluation of eyewitness testimony, it was not until the 1950s that the law began to make use of social and behavioural science research to inform its policy-making and to make judgements in individual cases. There then followed a growth in psychological research, some dealing with offending behaviour and some dealing with courtroom issues, and by the 1990s the term **forensic psychology** was increasingly being used to refer to the application of psychology to issues within the legal system. Bartol and Bartol (1999) suggest that forensic psychology:

> is both (a) the research endeavour that examines aspects of human behaviour directly related to the legal process (for example, eyewitness memory and testimony, jury decision making, or criminal behaviour), and (b) the professional practice of psychology with or in consultation with a legal system that encompasses both criminal and civil law and the numerous areas where they interact. Therefore, forensic psychology refers broadly to the production and application of psychological knowledge to the civil and criminal justice systems.
> (1999 p.3)

A forensic psychologist is therefore offering expertise across a broad range of issues, which might include evaluating offender treatment programmes, risk assessment in relation to parole decisions, expert testimony in relation to criminal cases or child custody decisions, advising the police on identifying burnout in their officers, or how best to negotiate with hostage takers. The important aspect of this definition, however, is the reliance on substantial academic research to inform any sort of advice the forensic psychologist can offer within the context of criminal or civil justice. This is why anyone seeking chartered status within the British Psychological Society as a forensic psychologist needs to demonstrate accredited academic and research competence in forensic psychology, together with a period of approved supervised practice in the field.

So, what questions do forensic psychologists attempt to provide a response to? Examples might include the following:

- Do people who commit crime think in different ways to people who don't?
- How successful are attempts to create psychological profiles of criminals?
- What are the most effective ways to police our communities?
- How confident can we be of testimony given in court?
- What are the real effects of punishment on offenders and their families?
- Can treatment programmes prevent future offending?
- Does the fear of crime match the reality?
- What are the psychological consequences of being a victim of crime?

How can we draw on psychology to provide the answers to these questions? Let's break it down into the recognisable fields of developmental psychology, cognitive psychology, social psychology, abnormal psychology and biological psychology, and identify some of the potential contributions.

Developmental psychology

We know that intellectual development can be impaired by a poor environment (including the foetal environment) and a lack of appropriate stimulation. This explains the success of programmes such as Operation Headstart in giving disadvantaged children an opportunity to succeed by influencing parental styles, teaching parents how to 'manage' their children's behaviour, giving positive reinforcement, shaping and modelling, and being consistent (Bee, 1995).

It is now widely accepted, thanks to the work of Bowlby (1944) on **maternal deprivation**, that young children need the opportunity to become emotionally attached to one or more caregivers, and to experience some continuity of care during childhood. Children who experience loss as a result of separation, divorce, parental mental illness, or bereavement, will need some form of counselling to help them come to terms with their feelings. Otherwise their psychological health may be jeopardised alongside their ability to form meaningful relationships in adulthood.

Children who display behavioural problems tend to come from families with harsh and inconsistent discipline patterns (Eron, Huesmann and Zelli, 1991). As a consequence they have not been able to develop parameters of appropriate behaviour. From a psychoanalytic perspective their superego has not developed normally. Alternatively, those children with behavioural problems may be suffering from Attention Deficit Hyperactivity Disorder (ADHD) which can be treated as long as the symptoms are recognised sufficiently early.

• **Figure 0.1:** Gender role socialisation: a little boy wearing armour and a little girl dressed as a fairy

Gender role socialisation is an important factor in childhood, as are traditional gender stereotypes which result in expectations of boys to be aggressive, controlling and independent, and girls to be polite and conforming. Boys' lower attainment at school and their higher incidence of learning problems can lead to over-compensation in other areas, e.g. minor offending, in order to achieve status and a clear identification with the male stereotype. Boys who take risks and behave impulsively are often popular at school, swots are rarely very popular, and peer pressure to take even more risks can be very difficult to resist. All the data suggests that being male is probably *the* most significant association with criminal behaviour.

Cognitive psychology

Our perceptions and thought processes influence our behaviour both directly and indirectly. When we choose to act in a particular way it is as a result of a costs–benefits analysis and a selection from our existing behavioural repertoire. Offending behaviour is no different in this sense to any other type of behaviour. This is why cognitive–behavioural treatment programmes are the most influential in terms of rehabilitation, because they tackle dysfunctional thought processes and belief systems and enable offenders to rebuild a more appropriate set of behavioural strategies.

As a consequence of memory research we are now aware that our systems for perceiving, storing and recalling information are susceptible to distortion at many levels. This has cast doubt on the accuracy of eyewitness testimony, but has also enabled the development of more effective strategies for interviewing witnesses, e.g. the cognitive interview. This uses a variety of mnemonic techniques to encourage witnesses to re-view and re-experience the event they witnessed without the interference of leading questions, resulting in improved recall.

Social psychology

Attribution theory suggests that when we ascribe meaning to behaviour (Why did Peter do that?) we tend to pay more attention to dispositional factors than to the context in which the behaviour occurs (Heider, 1958). For example, Peter fell over because he's clumsy, rather than Peter fell over because there was a banana skin there. These findings have important consequences for our investigation of criminal behaviour and the social context in which it occurs.

Our attitudes to authority can be easily manipulated, as Stanley Milgram (1973) showed, and so can the development of prejudice. Members of an out-group may feel their offending behaviour is justified because they have been oppressed, but their treatment may be disproportionately severe. Victims of hate crimes may be selected purely on the basis of ungrounded prejudice.

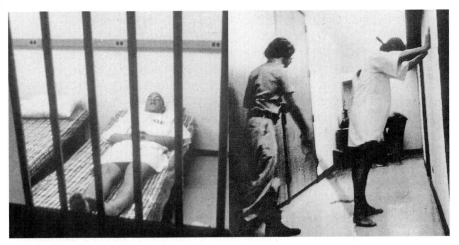

• **Figure 0.2:** Zimbardo's prisoners and guards study

Zimbardo *et al.* (1973) demonstrated quite convincingly in their 'prisoners and guards' study that we are all susceptible to internalising social roles and performing in accordance with the characteristics of these roles, even when we know them to be morally wrong. The process of deindividuation can also explain why some individuals behave in a group situation in ways which would normally be alien to them. During the critical period of adolescence, peer pressure and conformity to the norms of a delinquent group may produce uncharacteristic behaviour which has long-term negative consequences.

In the area of offender profiling, David Canter, Professor of Investigative Psychology at Liverpool University, emphasises that social interaction between offender and victim can provide crucial evidence about the likely identity of the offender. Canter suggests that the way an offender speaks to and behaves towards his or her victim will reveal personality patterns which also exist in the non-offending part of the offender's life.

Abnormal psychology

There is often a fine line between normality and abnormality, and the consequences of an inaccurate diagnosis of mental illness can be severe. However, the question of whether mentally ill offenders should be held responsible for their crimes has a long legal history. Problems with accurate diagnosis and judgements which are made about specific offences can interfere with any system which attempts equitable treatment. For instance, someone suffering from erotomania (an obsession with someone with whom the sufferer believes they have an intimate relationship) is statistically abnormal, is suffering from an identifiable mental illness, and therefore might qualify for psychiatric treatment. It is, however, only when their behaviour becomes threatening that this is regarded as a criminal offence which requires intervention. Stalking has only recently been recognised as criminal behaviour, and the courts currently seem unsure about how best to deal with it.

It has been sugested that up to 50% of the prison population meet the diagnostic criteria for **antisocial personality disorder** (APD), a term preferred by psychiatrists instead of labels such as psychopath or sociopath. APD is characterised by impulsivity, lying and manipulativeness, a lack of guilt, and a continuing tendency towards antisocial behaviour. Sufferers may appear to be quite normal because they have learned to play a particular role to get what they want, but whatever happens to them by way of punishment or disapproval they will continue to break the law without any apparent regard for others' feelings. Psychologists have developed scales to assess this condition, the most prominent of which is the Hare Psychopathy Checklist-Revised (PCL-R). However there is little agreement on the viability of treatment since APD sufferers are believed to be incapable of experiencing anxiety because of a dysfunctional autonomic system. The proposed system of dealing with these individuals by way of preventative detention is controversial, not least because issues of accurate diagnosis and risk assessment remain, as well as the question of human rights.

Biological psychology

The work of Chess and Thomas (1984) suggests that temperamental differences between individuals are present very soon after birth, and that these can influence interactions with parents, and consequently affect later behaviour. The legacy of genetic inheritance may have important consequences, but our awareness of these possibilities may enable us to intervene at a more appropriate time.

Whilst it has been suggested that crime 'runs in families' as a result of genetics, there is sufficient evidence of environmental influences to produce caution in this area. However, what does seem clear is that in some families a vulnerability is inherited which may or may not interact with environmental triggers to produce antisocial behaviour. Plomin (1994) suggests that neither genetic inheritance nor the environment are constants – even being brought up in the same family can be a very different experience for different individuals. Potential vulnerability can be spotted in early childhood behavioural indicators though, and this is where intervention should occur.

So, hopefully, the contribution of forensic psychology can be seen to be firmly rooted in the theoretical and methodological discipline of psychology, and its applications to the criminal justice system recognised not only for its current value but also its developing potential. An example of how psychological concepts have been applied to particular crimes, in this instance the Columbine High School shootings, can be found in Harrower (1999).

• **Figure 0.3:** Twin boys sharing the same genes but also the same environment

KEY TERMS

forensic psychology
gender role socialisation
attention deficit hyperactivity
disorder (ADHD)
maternal deprivation
attribution theory
antisocial personality disorder
(APD)

one

Explanations of criminal behaviour

Psychology is clearly not the only contributor to explanations of criminal behaviour, although in the past it has tended to be viewed as a rather simplistic and conservative contributor. This may be due to its emphasis on individual pathology, i.e. a search for deficits within the individual, and an apparent neglect of social factors in the construction of criminal careers. More recent developments in psychology, and particularly in the applied field of forensic psychology, however, have made a considerable impact on the contribution psychology as a discipline can make to our understanding of crime.

THIS CHAPTER EXAMINES:

- psychological theories of criminal behaviour
- individual and cultural differences in criminal behaviour
- the social context of crime.

What exactly is crime?

Before attempting an overview of the input of psychology, we need to take a step back and consider the problematic concept of crime itself. The question *what is crime?* sounds as if it should have obvious answers, and certainly there would probably be widespread agreement that some acts, such as personal violence or theft, constitute crimes the world over. However, there might be disagreement about whether these acts are still seen as crimes if the rule of law is challenged, for instance in wartime. It was only in 2001 that the mass rape of Muslim women during the Bosnian conflict of 1992–95 was first deemed to be a crime against humanity, with three of its perpetrators receiving lengthy prison sentences at the Hague War Tribunal. Prior to this, wartime rape and the provision of kidnapped 'comfort women' for soldiers had been regarded simply as a byproduct of war.

While legal sanctions hold, there is reasonable understanding about what constitutes crime, but this understanding tends to vary according to historical, cultural and power dimensions which may rule different behaviours as criminal at different times. Obvious examples of this are when laws change, so for example attempting suicide was regarded as a criminal offence until 1961, while incest was not classed as a crime until 1908. Similarly, female circumcision is acceptable in some cultures though not in the UK, while in contrast male circumcision has never been against the law, though in both cases genital mutilation occurs without the consent of the individual concerned.

Age and mental state also influence whether someone is regarded as having committed a crime. The age of criminal responsibility varies considerably from country to country, so in the UK it is 10 while in Norway it is 15. The murder of two small children by other children in both countries in 1993 and 1994 highlights the very different views taken of similar crimes. In 1993, two-year-old James Bulger was taken away from his mother in a Liverpool shopping centre by two boys aged ten who subsequently beat and murdered him. Both boys were charged with murder and appeared in an adult court more than a year later, when they were ordered to serve a minimum sentence of eight years. This was subsequently increased to ten and then fifteen years in response to public and media outrage, though this action was later deemed unlawful. During their time on remand they did not receive any psychiatric help because of their *not guilty* pleas, prompting one of the jurors to remark five years later:

> The trial was about retribution . . . It was apparent that in the dock were two children; almost entirely uncomprehending of most of the proceedings; distressed by those parts they did understand; subject to trial as if they were aware adults; unaccountably branded as 'evil' by the judge.
> (*The Guardian*, 5th November 1999, Letters)

In 1994 in Trondheim, Norway, a five-year-old girl was violently killed by three friends aged five and six while they were playing in the snow. There was no prosecution, the boys were not named in the media, and they were treated as victims rather than offenders. The police broke the news to the local community, appealing for their understanding, and people felt collective shame, grief and responsibility, not only for the victim and her family, but also for the boys and their families. The boys admitted what they had done and seemed shocked and afraid. They returned to school within a fortnight accompanied by a psychologist at all times and they received appropriate counselling, as did all the other children. The vast difference in the responses of these two communities to similar and horrendous crimes demonstrates not only the effect of media coverage of crime, but also the role of the state in determining how we all view offending behaviour, individual responsibility and the role of punishment.

Mentally ill offenders are not normally held responsible for their crimes unless it can be demonstrated that they intended to break the law. However, in many trials the distinction between offenders being presented as 'mad' or 'bad' has proved controversial and moved beyond simple psychiatric diagnosis into the realms of moral responsibility. For instance, Peter Sutcliffe murdered 13 women in the 1970s and his defence claimed diminished responsibility on the grounds that he was suffering from paranoid schizophrenia and heard voices telling him to kill prostitutes. The jury, however, decided that Sutcliffe was not sufficiently mentally ill to be absolved of responsibility for the murders; he was found guilty and sentenced to life imprisonment. Three years later he was transferred to a special hospital because of his mental illness. Similarly Jeffrey Dahmer, who murdered and cannibalised 17 young men in the 1980s, was found not to be suffering from the personality disorder and necrophilia his defence described, and was sent to prison, where he was murdered by another inmate in 1994. In both cases there was clear evidence of dysfunctional behaviour with psychiatric symptoms, and yet the horrific nature of the crimes seems to have demanded some form of public accountability and retribution.

● **Figure 1.1:** Serial killer Jeffrey Dahmer makes his initial court appearance in Milwaukee County Court with his lawyer, 25 July 1991. Dahmer is wearing the shirt of one of his 17 victims

Theories of criminal behaviour

Most theories attempting to explain criminal behaviour represent part of the classic psychological **nature versus nurture** debate: can behaviour be seen as the result of heredity or the effect of the environment?; are criminals *born* bad, or are they somehow *made* bad? Do offenders rationally choose to commit crime, or are they somehow programmed to do so? Genes are often said to set the limits on behaviour, while the environment shapes development within those limits. Thus a child born with some potential to offend may, depending upon their family environment, come to realise that potential or not. The discovery that our genetic make-up may not be as complex as was once believed suggests that the interaction between genetic vulnerability and environmental protection has become even more worthy of investigation.

Theme link to Perspectives and Issues (**the nature-nurture debate**)

Plomin (2001) suggests that behavioural genetics must become a prime component within the study of psychology in the future, not in the traditional and much criticised sense of genetic determinism but because 'behavioural genetic research provides the strongest available evidence for the importance of environmental factors'. (p.134) He adds that most behavioural disorders reveal some genetic influence, in fact rather more so than common medical disorders, but that the exact nature of the 'genotype–environment correlations' will require sensitive and sophisticated analysis. Intervention is then more likely to involve changes to the environment rather than genetic engineering.

All theories of criminal behaviour try to address the question of why people commit crime on the assumption that such a course of action merits explanation of the inexplicable, that criminals are somehow different from the rest of us, and that there might be a single cause of criminal behaviour. However, one of the major reasons offenders commit crime is simply because they enjoy it. Katz (1988) has spoken of the 'seductions of crime', while Hodge, McMurran and Hollin (1997) refer to criminal behaviour as an 'addiction'. Both perspectives recognise that the 'buzz' of risk, danger, fun, opportunism, status, and finanical gain merit serious examination. Joy-riding is a good example of the type of crime which can benefit from this sort of analysis – it is dangerous, temporary and very risky, yet extremely popular with young men (see Kilpatrick, 1997). This might be a useful avenue to explore alongside an assumption that there cannot be a monocausal or single explanation of criminal behaviour, because there are so many different types of offending. Also, most psychological research tells us that our behaviour, both rational and irrational, is a complex interaction between genetic, environmental, social and cultural factors.

Physiological, biological and genetic theories of crime

Some of these theories emphasise physical features, while others stress chromosomes, genetic transmission, or neurological factors, but they all place criminality firmly within the individual, playing down the possible influence of social factors. In other words, the reason someone is criminal is the result of internal or innate characteristics, rather than the consequence of being brought up in a poor environment. If we believe that criminals are very different to the rest of us, it is not too big a step to assume that they will also look quite different to the rest of us. Subsequent labelling and stereotyping can help us identify this group and reinforce our belief in their status as an out-group. Sheldon (1942) developed descriptions of three basic body types or **somatotypes** which he believed were correlated with particular types of personality. He suggested that broad and muscular mesomorphs were more likely to be criminals.

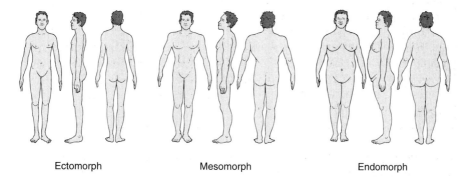

| Ectomorph | Mesomorph | Endomorph |

• **Figure 1.2:** Sheldon's body types with mesomorphs identified as the most likely criminals

Although Sheldon's work was criticised on methodological and subjective grounds – because he rated his subjects' body types himself, and assumed correlation was linked to causality – his theories were supported by Glueck and Glueck (1956). They found that 60% of their sample of delinquents were mesomorphs, while only 31% of their non-delinquent sample were, and Cortés and Gatti (1972) found in a sample of 100 delinquents that 57% were mesomorphic, compared with 19% of controls.

While these findings support the view that delinquents are likely to be muscular and fit, it remains unclear what the exact association might be between mesomorphy and crime. Boys tend to admire others who mature

Theme link to Perspectives and Issues (**individual differences**)

Following in the Ancient Greek tradition of physiognomy – judging people's character by studying their faces – William Sheldon (1942) suggested that there were three somatotypes with distinctive personality characteristics:

Endomorphs who are soft, round, comfort-loving, sentimental, tolerant and sociable while prone to depression.

Ectomorphs who are slender, fragile, sensitive, intellectual, solitary, restrained, and prone to schizophrenia.

Mesomorphs who are muscular, athletic, active, energetic, risk-takers, dominant and prone to delinquency.

early and are muscular and physically agile. The status these boys acquire can often only be maintained by taking risks, becoming involved in ever more daring and anti-social acts and increasing their chances of apprehension. This might explain their over-representation in delinquent samples, though mesomorphy is also associated with high testosterone levels (Hartl *et al.*, 1982).

We all tend to develop beliefs about what 'criminals' look like and this can determine our reactions to such people. Bull and McAlpine (1998) were able to demonstrate that these facial stereotypes can influence judgements of guilt, and clearly the stereotypes are often reinforced by media representations since casting editors tend to choose the same actors to portray villains. Could it be that we are not very nice to people whom we consider unattractive, and that over time these individuals begin to lose faith in themselves and act to fit their stereotype? Masters and Greaves (1969) surveyed the incidence of facial deformities in 11,000 prisoners and concluded that 60% of them had facial deformities, by comparison with 20% in a non-criminal population. This finding raises the possibility that some of these individuals turned to crime because of the social consequences of their disability.

Perhaps the most well-known explanation of crime which focuses on physical appearance is that of Cesare Lombroso, one of the founding fathers of criminology. In 1876 he published *L'Uomo Delinquente* in which he argued that criminals were genetically different from non-criminals, and this difference could literally be seen in people's faces. Lombroso suggested that criminals display a range of physical characteristics which reveal clues that they are **atavistic**, and this was tied to his belief in a linear evolutionary process with humans at the top end and animals at the bottom. His view of criminals was that they displayed features which had much in common with inferior animals lower down the evolutionary scale.

Dion, Berscheid and Walster (1972) found that people attributed more positive qualities to attractive people than to unattractive people. They were shown photographs and asked to rate people's personality characteristics on the basis of pictures alone. Their very favourable ratings of attractive people demonstrated the what-is-beautiful-is-also-good stereotype, whereby a halo effect seems to operate and assumptions are made on the basis of physical attributes alone. The stereotype seems to operate across a range of settings including the courtroom. Stewart (1980) found that judges were less likely to imprison attractive defendants than unattractive defendants, while Downs and Lyons (1991) showed that judges imposed lower fines on attractive defendants.

The criminal by nature has a feeble cranial capacity, a heavy and developed jaw, projecting (eye) ridges, an abnormal and asymmetrical cranium . . . projecting ears, frequently a crooked or flat nose. Criminals are subject to colour blindness, left-handedness is common, their muscular force is feeble.

Lombroso (1911) went so far as to suggest that the distinctive appearance of criminals was very similar to lower animals such as chimps, and that female offenders were biologically more like men than women.

But, in spite of the obvious criticism and lack of political correctness, could Lombroso have had something? Maybe we can rule out the possibility of

Lombroso's theories can be criticised on methodological grounds – for instance, he did not use a proper control group, often relying on large groups of soldiers, and his criminal samples contained large numbers of the mentally disturbed. One of the most important criticisms of Lombroso's theory was that he failed to recognise that correlation does not imply causality. Simply because his criminal subjects shared a significant number of physical anomalies does not mean that this made them criminal. It could be that poverty and deprivation produced the physical defects he noted, rather than them being the result of genetic transmission. In later years Lombroso modified his thinking on criminality and was more prepared to accept that the environment can influence the onset of criminal behaviour.

genetic transmission, for as Rowe (1990) says: 'No responsible geneticist would argue that a specific gene exists for crime, as specific genes may be identified for Huntington's disease or eye colour' (p.122) but we are now much more aware of the power of the media and its role in perpetuating stereotypes and self-fulfilling prophecies. If someone appears to fit our image of a 'criminal' do we assume the worst, and thereby create a social reality? Stereotypes certainly still appear to be exerting their influence. For instance, Lombroso suggested that the presence of tattoos was a good indicator of criminality; a recent study indicated that children were significantly more likely to pair a negative attribute with a drawing of a man with tattoos than one of a man without tattoos (Durkin and Houghton, 2000).

The 1960s saw the emergence of a new explanation of violent crime in terms of chromosomes and an identifiable genetic abnormality – the XYY syndrome. We all have 46 chromosomes in pairs, one of which determines our sex – XX for females, and XY for males. There is a variety of chromosomal abnormalities, one of which involves the presence of an extra Y chromosome in males, and is usually linked to above average height and low intelligence. The incidence of this condition in the general population is about 0.1%, but Price et al. (1966) found that 28% of the men in a Scottish State Hospital for the criminally insane were XYY. The assumption was that individuals with an extra Y chromosome must somehow be 'supermales' and therefore more inclined towards violence, hence their over-representation in prisons and special hospitals (Jarvik et al., 1973). The XYY defence was used in some criminal trials, and suggestions were made that mass screening be carried out to detect these individuals at an early age, in order to take preventative action.

However, a comprehensive Danish study which screened 4591 men for the presence of XYY found only 12 cases (Witkin *et al.*, 1976). While these individuals were indeed more likely to be involved in crime (41.7% of them, by comparison with 9.3% of the XY individuals), it was not involvement in violent crime. Their conclusion was that the over-representation of XYY males in prisons and special hospitals was more likely to be the result of other, visible characteristics – low intelligence and above-average height – and the social reaction that these characteristics may have produced, rather than genetic predisposition for crime.

DOES CRIME RUN IN FAMILIES?

Contemporary researchers have searched for support for the **genetic transmission** of crime by studying criminal families, and the possibility that criminal tendencies are inherited. Earlier researchers had claimed this was so by looking at the family trees of criminals, and although these studies can be criticised for their lack of methodological rigour, subsequent studies have shown that a relatively small number of offenders, often from the same family, tend to be chronic repeat offenders across a significant time period

(Farrington, 1997). Is this the result of prejudice, years of social deprivation, or genetic transmission, and why are the effects only experienced by a minority of individuals, often young males?

A consistent research finding confirms that criminal parents are indeed more likely to have criminal children, for example Osborn and West (1979) found that 40% of the sons of criminal fathers had criminal convictions, compared with 13% for the sons of non-criminal fathers. However, this does not provide evidence for genetic transmission, since 60% of those who had criminal fathers did not go on to become criminals themselves. Other factors must be involved in the process, which is why studying families provides rich but often complex data about the interaction between biological and social influences.

Some of these other influencing factors within the family could be lifestyle, poverty, family size or parenting styles, and one of the most influential longitudinal studies of the development of criminal behaviour examined these factors over a 30 year period. David Farrington and his colleagues collected data on a regular basis from a sample of working-class boys and their families, in order to see which of them became delinquent. They discovered that 20% of their sample had criminal convictions by the age of 17, and that 50% of all the convictions recorded had been acquired by only 5% of the boys. Within this group of repeat offenders Farrington (1997) notes that there were early indicators of potential problems. These boys had been described as troublesome or dishonest in primary school, came from poorer, larger families, were more likely to have criminal parents, and had experienced harsh or erratic parenting. Farrington suggests that from his own study and other comparable studies there are:

> numerous replicable predictors of delinquency over time and place, including impulsivity, attention problems, low school attainment, poor parental supervision, parental conflict, an antisocial parent, a young mother, large family size, low family income, and coming from a broken family.
>
> (1997 p.363)

Significantly, however, Farrington states that having a convicted parent is more likely to be related to persistency or continuity of offending rather than early onset. This suggests that criminal behaviour develops within a social context of inappropriate role models and dysfunctional reward patterns, rather than being a direct result of genetic transmission. There is also a gender connection here, since the girls in the families studied did not develop criminal careers in the way that their brothers were prone to do.

A well-established method for exploring the potential genetic component of a number of characteristics including criminality is that of **twin studies**. This is on the assumption that because monozygotic (MZ) or identical twins share the same genes, while dizygotic (DZ) or non-identical twins share about 50% of

Summary of Farrington's findings

- a longitudinal study of 411 boys born in the East End in 1953
- 20% had acquired convictions by age 17
- 33% had acquired convictions by age 25
- 50% of the total convictions had been acquired by < 6% of the sample, i.e. 23 boys
- most of these chronic offenders shared common childhood characteristics:
  - rated troublesome/dishonest in primary school
  - came from poorer, larger families
  - more likely to have criminal parents
  - experienced harsh/erratic parental discipline, and family conflict
- at age 10
  - identified as hyperactive, impulsive, unpopular, low intelligence
- at age 14
  - aggressive, with delinquent friends
- at age 18
  - drank more, smoked more, gambled
  - had tattoos, bitten nails, a low pulse rate
  - associated with gangs
- at age 32
  - poorer housing
  - marital break-up
  - psychiatric disorder
  - problems with own children

their genes (just like any other siblings), any similarities between twin pairs can be distinguished as the result of genetic or environmental influences. Unfortunately the issues are not quite as simple as this: when twins have been studied in relation to criminality, and it has been found that MZ twin pairs appear to share more criminal tendencies than do DZ twins, it has been argued that this demonstrates a significant genetic component in criminal behaviour (for example Christiansen, 1977).

However, all twin studies tend to suffer from the same difficulties, which makes interpreting their results problematic. For instance, MZ twins look alike, and may therefore generate more similar social responses than DZ twins. This means that in addition to sharing the same genes, they may share an almost identical environment too. They are also likely to share the same interests, which might include criminal behaviour, and as MZ twins are always the same sex while DZ twins are not, it could be that the lower concordance rate for DZ twin pairs is explained by a preponderance of males in the MZ pairs.

Psychologists investigate the possible influence of genetics by studying pairs of identical and non-identical twins. If it is found that identical twins are more similar than non-identical twins then this would suggest a strong genetic influence. The extent of difference is measured by looking at 'concordance', or the degree to which twins display the same behaviour or characteristics. This is usually expressed as a percentage, so a 100% concordance would indicate that in every pair studied both twins possessed the same characteristic, while a 50% concordance would indicate that in half of the total sample both members of a twin pair displayed the same behaviour.

In the absence of crime-related data on MZ twins reared apart and therefore sharing nothing but genes, it is difficult to draw any conclusions, though it is worth noting that recent studies looking at measures of personality and intelligence in MZ twin pairs who were reared apart found some striking similarities, which suggest that the genetic component is not insignificant (Bouchard, Lykken, McGue, Segal and Tellegen, 1990).

An alternative approach to determining the extent of possible genetic influence is to study adopted children – this allows examination of the extent of biological inheritance together with that of the environment in the adoptive home. If the behaviour of adopted children is more similar to their biological parents than to their adoptive parents, this would provide strong support for genetic transmission.

In one of the early adoption studies looking at criminal behaviour, Crowe (1974) found that in a sample of 52 adopted children of imprisoned women, seven of them had at least one criminal conviction, by comparison with only one in a matched control group. Subsequent studies have supported these findings. For example, Mednick, Gabrielli and Hutchings (1987) found that boys whose biological parent had a criminal record were more likely to have been convicted of a crime than were boys whose adoptive parent had been convicted. Thus, the biological parents' genetic contribution had a greater effect on behaviour than did the adoptive parents' rearing. When Walters (1992) carried out a meta-analysis of 13 adoption studies he found a moderate but significant association between hereditary variables and crime, which led him to suggest that the individual genetic inheritance of criminal behaviour is 11–17%. Some of the possible interaction effects between genes and the environment are highlighted by Bohman's (1995) findings overleaf.

Bohman (1995) found that there was more chance of criminality where there was a genetic risk factor *together* with an environmental risk factor. The environment clearly seemed to have its most marked effect on those children who might have already been genetically vulnerable.

<u>Rates of criminal conviction in adopted children (Bohman, 1995)</u>

	Adoptive parents had criminal record	Adoptive parents had no criminal record
Biological parents had criminal record	40%	12%
Biological parents had no criminal record	7%	3%

Adoption studies are fraught with the same problems as twin studies, in that adoptive families are often selected on the basis of their similarity to the original family, while not all children are adopted at birth, so disentangling the effects of genetic and environmental influences can be difficult.

When researchers look for neurological explanations of criminal behaviour they often find significant influences, but these tend to relate to specific types of offending, such as violent behaviour, or particular episodes of offending which result from identifiable influences, such as brain damage or drug abuse. Alcohol acts as a **disinhibitor**, depressing the normal mechanisms which control socially inappropriate behaviour, while Prozac can produce akathisia, a state of restlessness and unease which can lead to suicide or violence against others (Healy, 1997). The brain is a vulnerable organ and can be susceptible to a range of influences, although these may not be obvious at the time. For instance, when Charles Whitman killed 21 people during one day in 1966, shooting 16 of them from a Texas university tower, an autopsy subsequently revealed that he had a large brain tumour which was affecting the area of the brain responsible for controlling aggressive urges, the amygdala. Testosterone can also affect the activity of neurotransmitters in the brain, lowering serotonin levels,creating a neurological state which is associated with disinhibition, acting on impulse and seeking arousal and stimulation in the environment.

Another suggestion is that certain individuals, as a result of brain damage at birth, suffer from a cluster of symptoms which render them incapable of moral control, and are constantly seeking stimulation because of this cortical under-arousal. The symptoms appear in early childhood, are subsumed in the term Attention Deficit Hyperactivity Disorder (ADHD), and include an

Some authors have argued strongly that genetics play a major role in determining criminality (Raine, 1993), to the extent that screening has been suggested in order to identify potential criminals at an early age. However, the complexity of the interaction between nature and nurture, together with the political ramifications, should demand caution in the interpretation and application of these research findings.

inappropriate degree of inattention, impulsiveness, challenging behaviour and hyperactivity. Moir and Jessel (1995) have suggested that this disorder can account for impulsive and seemingly irrational crimes, some of which involve violence. Moreover, they suggest that brain scans could identify the disorder in young children who are already showing behavioural problems, and that treatment with Ritalin (a stimulant which can reduce the need for sensation and arousal) together with parental training might prevent these children from growing up to be seriously anti-social. The jury is out on this disorder and its treatment, however, with serious concern expressed about early and inaccurate diagnosis, inappropriately high doses of medication, and potentially damaging labelling. For example, labelling a small child as suffering from a medical condition said to be linked with adult violent crime may lead to stigma and isolation.

PSYCHOLOGICAL THEORIES OF CRIME

An unusual explanation of crime which attempts to combine genetic, biological and psychological factors was offered by Hans Eysenck (1964), and refined by Eysenck and Gudjonsson (1989). While it is often presented as a general theory of crime it actually attempts to explain why some people fail to follow rules, and suggests that neuroticism and extroversion are linked to antisocial behaviour.

At a later stage in the development of his theory Eysenck introduced a third personality variable – P (psychoticism) – which he believed was marked by aggressive, cold and impersonal behaviour. He believed high scorers on this scale, together with high extraversion and neuroticism scores, would be more likely to be associated with violent crime.

Much research has been generated in an attempt to verify Eysenck's theory (see Blackburn, 1993), and while there has been some support for an association between psychoticism and serious criminal behaviour, there has been little support for the predicted configuration of high scores in extraversion, neuroticism and psychoticism. Moreover, there has been serious criticism of the authority with which this particular theory has been presented when there are misgivings about any evidence for its theoretical foundation

Eysenck developed measures of **introversion/extraversion** and **neuroticism/stability** to characterise personality, believing that most people would score somewhere in the middle of each of these two scales. Neuroticism was seen to include characteristics such as low self-esteem, emotionality, and a tendency to depression and anxiety, while extraversion was signalled by sociability, impulsivity, a search for excitement, and optimism.

Eysenck believed that some people are born with different types of autonomic nervous systems which will determine they way they react to environmental stimuli. The extravert is under-aroused and therefore searches the environment for stimulation, while also being resistant to conditioning. Similarly neurotic individuals have a labile autonomic nervous system, are difficult to condition because of their anxiety and will react strongly to unpleasant stimuli. High scores on both of these dimensions – extraversion and neuroticism – were thought to increase the probablility of offending behaviour and resistance to socialisation.

Eysenck believed that personality is largely determined by genetic factors, and that certain personality types are inclined towards crime. He described these individuals within his own classification system as neurotic extraverts who, because of their genetic inheritance, are unlikely to have learned the rules of social behaviour which most children acquire through the process of socialisation. Their high score on the extraversion scale means that they are under-aroused, impulsive and outgoing sensation-seekers who are difficult to condition. High neuroticism scores are said to be linked with moodiness, anxiety and depression, which produces a resistance to social conditioning and an inability to learn from mistakes.

(Trasler, 1987). The suggested link between crime and specific personality types does, however, have some intuitive strength. Those individuals who are labelled as psychopaths, or as suffering from antisocial personality disorder, will have shown a resistance to conditioning from an early age, as well as the sort of personality characteristics which are likely to produce conflict.

PSYCHOANALYTIC THEORIES OF CRIME

An alternative explanation of criminal tendencies, linked to the characteristics Eysenck associated with psychoticism but which relate more appropriately to psychopathy, is that of John Bowlby (1944). Bowlby suggested that any disruption of the attachment bond between mother and child in the early years might lead to later deviance, mainly because of the consequent inability of

• **Figure 1.3:** Being scolded should help the child develop a sense of right and wrong – a conscience

such a child to develop any meaningful relationships. This psychodynamic theory of 'maternal deprivation' led to serious concerns about the quality of mothering especially in the case of children whose mothers worked, and in spite of the potent critique provided by, amongst others, Rutter (1971), continued to hold currency in explanations of juvenile delinquency for a considerable period of time.

Bowlby's work is very much rooted in a psychoanalytic framework, and although Freud himself had little to say about crime, his view of the small child as inherently asocial and motivated by pleasure-seeking and self-destructive impulses is used and developed by Bowlby, in order to explain adult criminal behaviour. If the child is raised in a dysfunctional family it may cause long-term damage to their superego or conscience. A poorly developed superego will result in a lack of control over anti-social impulses, impulsiveness and a lack of guilt, leading to unacceptable behaviour. In contrast, an over-developed superego will produce a desire for punishment, unresolved guilt, and a subsequent 'acting out' type of behaviour.

While psychoanalytic explanations hold some intuitive strength, their emphasis that crime develops from unconscious conflicts in childhood does not square with the idea that some criminal behaviour involves rational planning. Moreover, one of the essential assumptions of psychoanalytic theory is that females develop an inferior superego/conscience and should therefore be more likely to commit crime, a view which is simply not borne out by crime statistics.

Clarke and Clarke (1998) suggest that there has been undue emphasis on the irrevocably negative consequences of early deprivation, and point to case studies where children who have suffered severe disadvantages have been able to make remarkable recoveries, for example those described by Koluchova (1991). The possibility of compensation exists, although Clarke and Clarke do say that one of the consequences of adverse early experience is a degree of vulnerability which could result in regression should further stress occur.

Theme link to Perspectives and Issues (**developmental psychology**)

Koluchova (1991) describes twin boys whose mother died shortly after birth and who were fostered for a year before being returned to their father who had remarried. The step-mother kept them in the cellar for five years, and when they were discovered at the age of seven they had no speech, their growth had been stunted, and they had rickets. Doctors who examined them predicted permanent psychological and physical damage, but following adoption both boys made a complete recovery and were successful in their adult lives. This case highlights the potential for some children in certain contexts to reverse the effects of even severe early deprivation.

SOCIAL LEARNING THEORIES OF CRIME

A stronger contender in the stakes of psychological explanations of crime is **social learning theory**. Within this theory crime is seen as a product of learning, or as a failure of the socialisation process which endeavours to teach children how to behave appropriately. Children usually learn socially acceptable behaviour by acquiring an association of fear or anxiety with anti-social acts which prevents them from behaving similarly in the future. Trasler (1978) suggests that ineffective parental strategies may produce inadequately socialised children who then go on to offend. This is particularly likely if these children also associate with other children from whom they learn offending patterns of behaviour.

The view that criminal behaviour, in common with all other behaviour, is a learned response was most clearly expressed by Sutherland (1939) in his theory of 'differential association'. Sutherland suggested that individuals learn criminal behaviour by becoming part of close groups for whom offending has become a norm. Not only are criminal skills acquired, but also attitudes and beliefs which support offending behaviour, together with a feeling of group identity and belonging.

Sutherland was describing powerful social forces working on the individual and affecting skills, attitudes and beliefs. His theory was in many ways ahead of its time in representing a very definite move away from a view of criminals as predisposed to a life of crime. He also attempted an analysis of the gender differential in crime, arguing that boys are more likely to become delinquent than girls because they are less strictly controlled, and are taught to be aggressive and active risk-seekers, all characteristics likely to bring success in the criminal world.

Theme link to Perspectives and Issues (**reinforcement**)

Subsequent developments of Sutherland's theory emphasise the role of rewards and punishments, learning by imitation, and observation of others' behaviour, as outlined by Bandura (1977). Peers who are held in high regard are very influential role models, as are media stars, while rewards which might encourage certain behaviours include status, self-esteem, financial incentives or just plain excitement.

One aspect of social learning theory which has been developed as a possible explanation of violent behaviour is exposure to violence on television, in films, video and computer games. The influence is ascribed to imitation, but also desensitisation, with viewers observing so much violence on screen that they begin to see such behaviour as normal. Over 5,000 articles on the possible link between media violence and aggression have so far been published (Wallbott, 1996), but it has not been possible to conclusively demonstrate a causal link between the two, or to explain why some individuals copy screen actions while the vast majority do not.

SOCIAL AND CULTURAL FACTORS

It would seem that negative experiences at school are often linked with delinquency, and that in many ways the school acts as a catalyst for pre-existing problems (Hirschi, 1969). Low academic achievement is a characteristic of many offenders but this is not to say that poor intellectual skills are the contributing factor. It may be that particular schools fail to engage with challenging pupils who then opt out of the school system, play truant, and become involved in offending behaviour, failing to achieve the educational qualifications they may need to escape the spiral into a criminal career. Hargreaves (1980) identifies the features of a school which may contain high numbers of delinquent pupils and these include high staff turnover, low staff commitment, streaming, social disadvantage, and a view of pupils as being of low ability.

More black pupils are excluded from school and this leads to the assumption that black people, particularly young black men, are disproportionately involved in crime, a view often supported by media coverage of crime. Official data and self-report studies would bear this out, in addition to the disproportionate likelihood of black people also being the victims of crime. For instance, 12% of arrests in 1998–99 were of non-white individuals (7% black, 4% Asian, 1% other), but relative to the population this was four times the rate of arrests of white people (Home Office, 2000). However, as Feldman (1993) points out, the picture is not as clear-cut as the official data suggest, and in relation to some crime the actual number of offences committed by blacks and whites is similar. The major difference is that significantly more blacks are likely to commit at least one offence, possibly casual, whereas individual whites are more likely to be persistent or chronic offenders.

In Britain and America a higher proportion of people of Afro-Caribbean and black African origin are in prison than other ethnic groups. Is this because different ethnic groups are treated unequally in the criminal justice system, or are rates of crime higher amongst certain ethnic minority groups? In 1999 18% of the prison population was made up of non-whites (12% black, 3% Asian, 3% other) (Home Office, 2000). The research evidence suggests that black people are indeed treated unequally within criminal justice processes, but the differential in imprisonment rates is said by some to be the result of higher crime rates among black people (Wilbanks, 1987). Reiner (1993) argues that methodological flaws beset any attempt to provide rational explanations of the differences in crime rates and imprisonment rates, and that it is still possible to argue that black crime is partially the result of white racism.

While some have suggested that blacks are more likely to be involved in crime because of genetic inferiority (Rushton, 1990), it is clear that a more likely explanation lies in the sub-culture of violence and social disadvantage which many black people share, and institutional racism within the criminal justice system. Racial discrimination undoubtedly limits the educational and occupational opportunities available to ethnic minorities, and there are biases operating in the legal processing of offenders which work against black people. These biases appear to be remarkably resistant to intervention, despite the findings of the 1999 Stephen Lawrence enquiry.

WHY IS GENDER IMPORTANT IN EXPLANATIONS OF CRIME?

Probably the most significant feature of both recorded and self-reported crime is that more males than females commit offences. This is particularly true for violent crime, in spite of claims that women are becoming more aggressive (Krista, 1994), or that, because of their inherent deviousness, they have always been more criminal but have simply been able to conceal it (Pollak, 1950). In 1997 only 17% of known offenders were women, and it is estimated that only

8% of women have a conviction by the age of 40, compared with 34% of men (Home Office, 1999). There have also been suggestions that the criminal justice system is more 'chivalrous' towards females, and thus the gender difference is not as large as would appear from official figures (Hedderman and Hough, 1994), although self-report studies bear out the differential (Hindelang, 1979).

Most explanations of the gender gap in crime draw on accepted differences between males and females such as dominance, aggression, physique and nurturance. Others point to female socialisation which tends to be characterised by greater parental supervision, more stress on conformity, and fewer opportunities for crime. Those females who do deviate are viewed as having not only rejected society's rules but the traditional female role too, and are described as showing 'double deviance' while risking 'double jeopardy' (Heidensohn, 1995). In fact Lombroso and Ferrero (1895) suggested that criminal women were rare, but those who had not been 'neutralised by maternity' were likely to become even worse criminals than men.

Criminology has notoriously ignored the issue of gender, preferring to offer universal theories of crime based on empirical work which has relied only on male subjects. As Cain (1989) points out:

> Men as males have not been the objects of the criminological gaze. Yet the most consistent and dramatic findings from Lombroso to post-modern criminology is not that most criminals are working-class ... but that most criminals are, and always have been, men. (p.4)

It was not until the 1970s that feminist criminologists such as Heidensohn (1968) and Smart (1977) began to point out this gross oversight. Since then there have been significant developments in the area, with calls to 'feminize' socialisation in an attempt to reduce crime and to ascertain why females tend to conform rather than searching for why males offend (Heidensohn, 1995); and suggestions that 'masculinity' itself should be examined more closely in order to understand why so many young men commit offences and are also the victims of crime (Messerschmidt, 1993; Newburn and Stanko, 1994; Walklate, 2001). As Wilson and Herrnstein (1985) observe:

> Crime is an activity disproportionately carried out by young men living in large cities. There are old criminals, and female ones, and rural and small town ones, but to a much greater degree than would be expected by chance, criminals are young urban males. (p.26)

The fact that over 80% of all offenders are male (Home Office, 1999), and that this pattern is repeated internationally, inevitably begs the question that many criminologists have hitherto avoided asking – what is it about the cultural history and social construction of *masculinity* which ensures that so many young men become involved in crime? One of the most useful analyses of masculinity in relation to crime has come from theorists using the concepts of psychoanalysis and object-relations theory in an attempt to place psychic processes within a social context. Frosh (1994) draws on the work of Nancy Chodorow (1978), and argues that the process of separation in early childhood is different for girls and boys, and that while girls may be left with the problem of achieving independence and self-esteem, boys are left with an ambivalence towards women and commitment which scars all their future attempts to achieve success in personal relationships. They strive towards a socially defined masculinity, but this masculinity brings with it a terrible cost, namely a culture of violence. To be a real man involves being harsh, cold, punitive and callous, in order to achieve power and acceptance. If that power is not immediately available there will be resentment and a desire for revenge. Male-on-male violence is often justified in terms of negotiations about hierarchies of masculinity: teaching someone a lesson, saving face, or controlling territory (see Tomsen, 1997). Fights are seen as an acceptable means of resolving disputes, preserving and reinforcing status, even resolving insecurity about status. This degree of violence then becomes 'normal', and begins to permeate all relationships (Jefferson and Carlen, 1996).

Rather than simply examining female crime as if it were somehow different – and in so doing accepting a marginalised status within criminology which allows the discipline's gender-blindness to be condoned and continue – it is suggested that a gendered analysis of crime is the only way forward. Messerschmidt (1993) provides an astute analysis of gender and crime, highlighting particular aspects of masculinity, such as the collective processes of male youth groups and the 'public' arena in which masculine rituals are played out, as the major contributory factors to the predominance of male crime.

There have also been some very useful attempts to provide gendered analyses of specific crimes, including Jackson's (1995) examination of the murder of James Bulger, and Mai and Alpert's (2000) psychodynamic analysis of the motives of the two young men involved in the Colombine High School shootings. In both accounts links are made between the social construction of masculinity, the masculine signifier of violence, and the potential mismatch between cultural expectations and vulnerable individuals which may lead to inappropriate overcompensation.

Summary

Psychological explanations of crime reflect the range of perspectives within the discipline of psychology. Thus, psychobiological, psychoanalytic and learning theories are well represented, alongside a predictable emphasis on individual differences. However, crime always occurs in a social context and so factors such as ethnicity, gender, group dynamics, media pressure and cultural expectations cannot be ignored. The contribution of psychology is therefore valuable in terms of extending our understanding of crime as long as it is seen as part of a multidisciplinary approach.

KEY TERMS

nature versus nurture debate
somatotypes
atavistic
genetic transmission
twin studies and concordance
disinhibitors
introversion/extraversion
neuroticism/stability
early deprivation
social learning theory
masculinity

EXERCISE 1

Most people are familiar with the murder of 2-year-old James Bulger by Robert Thompson and Jon Venables, both aged 10 at the time of the murder. Ask a group of young adults what they think of Thompson and Venables and whether they were punished sufficiently. They may well suggest that the two boys weren't punished enough in view of the dreadful nature of their crime. Then ask them whether they would feel differently if Thompson or Venables was their son or brother.

The anger many people feel towards Thompson and Venables stems from the understandable sympathy they feel for James Bulger and his parents. However, Thompson and Venables were children too – who was there to care for them?

EXERCISE 2

List all the factors which have been said to contribute to the development of offending behaviour, for example brain damage, drugs, peer group pressure, etc. Then list all the different types of offending, for example violence, fraud, vandalism, car theft, etc. To what extent can each of the explanations 'match' the crime types?

EXERCISE 3

1. (a) Describe one biological explanation of crime, and one social explanation of crime.
   (b) Evaluate the extent to which each explanation is viable.

2. Discuss the suggestion that masculinity is significantly associated with criminal activity.

two

Criminal thinking patterns

In this chapter the emphasis shifts to asking why offenders *consider* committing crime, and whether there is something distinctive about their thinking patterns which facilitates a suspension of the social controls which the majority of people observe. We will examine:

- morality and crime
- social cognition and crime
- rationality and choice in determining involvement in crime.

In contrast to **determinist theories** of crime which presuppose offenders are passively driven to commit offences, **rational choice theories** of crime focus on the cognitive aspects of offending. Rational choice theories adopt a perspective whereby offenders are seen to think about their actions and exercise a judgement as to whether the risk of detection is outweighed by the potential reward before they choose to offend (Cornish & Clarke, 1986). This can be seen as an information processing approach which assumes that offenders make rational decisions about the benefits of criminal behaviour after collecting and evaluating all the relevant information. Van Den Haag (1982) expresses the concept of rational choice very clearly:

> I do not see any relevant difference between dentistry and prostitution or car theft, except that the latter do not require a license ... The frequency of rape, or of mugging, is essentially determined by the expected comparative net advantage, just as is the rate of dentistry and burglary. The comparative net advantage consists in the satisfaction (produced by the money or by the violative act itself) expected from the crime, less the expected cost of achieving it, compared to the net satisfaction expected from other activities in which the offender has the opportunity to engage. Cost in the main equals the expected penalty divided by the risk of suffering it. (1982 p.1026–07)

In spite of its intuitive appeal which chimes with more theoretical emphasis on **free will** together with the possibility of changing criminal thinking patterns, there are some inherent difficulties with rational choice theory. For instance, not all offending decisions are rational. Thus while the theory may be useful in relation to crimes which require planning such as burglary or fraud, or where there is a time frame during which information can be evaluated, it does not fit as well with the impulsive crimes that many young men commit (Crawford, 1998). It could be argued that rationality is also limited in some circumstances, for instance when an offender is mentally disturbed or under the influence of alcohol. Moreover, when offenders are completing their cost–benefit analysis they may not be in full possession of all the facts or the true likelihood of apprehension, so their decisions in these circumstances, cannot necessarily be viewed as rational.

A major difficulty, however, is the finding that offenders at different stages of their criminal career will tend to judge crime opportunities differently, and may also take into account previous experiences of punishment. This weakens any general theory of crime which attempts to explain offending in terms of its onset or beginning, its perseverance or continuation, and its end. Thus Carroll and Weaver (1986) found that when they analysed offenders' verbalised thoughts during crime simulations, experienced shoplifters were adept at evaluating opportunities for offending but used the information selectively, while novice shoplifters focused on the major question of whether to offend at all. Their cognitive processes were thus utilised quite differently, and the concepts of rationality and choice were shown to be problematic.

Theme link to Perspectives and Issues (**determinism**)

Determinist theories assume that offenders are predisposed towards criminal behaviour, whether the cause of these tendencies is social, biological or psychological. However, those who support a free will perspective argue that our actions are essentially rational, and even if the criminal chooses to offend because s/he is motivated by self-interest, this is still a rational decision.

Yochelson and Samenow (1976) also focus on cognitive processes but emphasise the role of **cognitive dysfunction** in criminal behaviour. The concept of rationality therefore disappears. They suggest that criminals have quite distinct and erroneous 'thinking patterns' which differentiate them from non-criminals. From their interviews with 240 male offenders they conclude that criminals may be less intelligent than non-criminals but they are essentially in control of their lives and their criminality is the result of choices made from an early age. Yochelson and Samenow emphasise cognitive processes which lead to a distorted self-image and result not only in criminal choices but a denial of responsibility. They identify 40 'thinking errors' made by criminals, the errors falling into three categories:

- *Criminal thinking patterns* which are characterised simultaneously by fear and a need for power and control. Other features include a search for perfection, lying, and inconsistencies or fragmentation of thinking.
- *Automatic thinking errors* which include a lack of empathy and trust, a failure to accept obligations, and a secretive communication style.
- *Crime-related thinking errors* which include optimistic fantasising about specific criminal acts with no regard for deterrent factors.

Yochelson and Samenow are suggesting therefore that criminals are not necessarily impulsive, that they will have planned and fantasised about their actions, and it is these thinking patterns which need to be confronted in treatment. Wulach (1988) however, has criticised their approach, pointing out that Yochelson and Samenow are simply describing psychopaths and their theory cannot therefore be regarded as a general theory of crime.

The area of **social cognition** is likely to be more fruitful for an investigation into criminal thinking, if only because of the acknowledgement of the role of free will together with the learning component. This component explains the development of particular aspects of social cognition which might contribute towards criminal activity, including moral reasoning, empathy, impulsivity and locus of control.

Some theorists see criminal behaviour as a failure of appropriate **moral development** and retarded moral reasoning. Conformity to society's rules comes about through the process of socialisation when individuals internalise these rules as a result of conditioning, modelling and identification. The main providers of directions will normally be parents, but teachers and friends also play a part. The assumption is that none of us would naturally want to follow these rules as we are instinctively asocial (Freud's view), but in order to avoid punishment and to obtain rewards (such as being accepted and not ostracised) we learn to distinguish between right and wrong. In other words we develop a conscience or 'superego'. Both Piaget (1959) and Kohlberg (1976) challenge this view, arguing that moral development is guided by cognitive needs and a wish to understand the reality of the world (one in which most people do conform). They suggest that children engage in social interactions and then actively construct moral beliefs, rather than simply accepting moral rules handed down by others. This process occurs within the normal sequential process of cognitive development outlined by Piaget (1959). Thus initially children will view adult rules as fixed and unchangeable, and then gradually begin to see rules as the product of group discussion and agreement.

Kohlberg (1976) expands Piaget's theory of cognitive development to include three levels of moral reasoning, each of which has two stages. Kohlberg argues that everyone proceeds through these stages in the same order, and that progression is dependent on appropriate levels of cognitive development, which explains why not everyone achieves Level 3.

Theme link to Perspectives and Issues (**developmental psychology**)

Kohlberg's theory of moral development focuses on the relationship between the self and society's rules, but relies on Piaget's stage theory of cognitive development.

Level 1 – Preconventional
This level parallels concrete operational thinking so it typifies pre-adolescents who have not yet developed their own personal code of morality, accepting instead adult standards but also taking into account the likely consequences of rule-breaking.

Level 2 – Conventional
The majority of adolescents and adults achieve this level and begin to internalise the moral standards of valued role models. They are also able to judge morality from the perspective of the group or society.

Level 3 – Postconventional
This level is only reached by the minority of adults who achieve formal operational thought. They understand societal rules in terms of higher moral principles and the need for democratically agreed rules. At the very highest stage, however, they may feel it appropriate to follow their conscience, even if this means breaking rules.

Kohlberg developed his theory as a result of presenting hypothetical moral dilemmas to mostly male participants, asking them how they would react and why. He then rated their responses within a hierarchical framework. Kohlberg's theory assumes reason rather than impulse as an explanation of criminal behaviour and its emphasis on cognitive processes moves it away from determinism, but his theory has been criticised for being both ethnocentric and gender-biased. The universal moral principles on which the theory rests may be typical of Western societies, but are not necessarily held by other cultures (Eckensberger, 1994). Moreover, Carol Gilligan (1982) has strongly argued that Kohlberg's theory places a higher value on male morality based on abstract principles, while devaluing female morality based on principles of care and compassion. As a result of this differential evaluation women are rated lower than men when Kohlberg's moral dilemmas are used for testing moral development. The major weakness of Kohlberg's theory in relation to crime, however, is that it is essentially a theory about moral thinking rather than an explanation of criminal behaviour. What we say we might do in a hypothetical situation does not necessarily match what we actually do.

Nonetheless attempts have been made to discover whether young offenders display lower levels of moral development, or at least developmental delay, using Kohlberg's paradigm. This has been found to be the case in some studies with the majority of offenders functioning at Stage 2 of Level 1 (Thornton, 1987; Palmer and Hollin, 2000). It has been suggested that this delay could be the result of a lack of opportunity within the family for the development of problem-solving abilities. Mears *et al.* (1998) also investigate the gender gap in delinquency, comparing the influence of peer pressure and moral evaluations of behaviour and drawing on the work of Sutherland and Gilligan. Despite the findings from some studies that many offenders do function at the conventional level, and that only persistent or psychopathic offenders remain in the preconventional level (Kegan, 1986), training programmes have been developed which endeavour to raise the level of moral development in young offenders by helping them reduce their egocentricity or their tendency to view the world from their own standpoint only. This is accomplished by providing opportunities for moral discussion and role-taking (Gordon and Arbuthnot, 1987), though the most successful approach to treatment which draws on cognitive psychology is the *Reasoning and Rehabilitation Project* developed by Ross, Fabiano and Ewles (1988). This approach focuses on the development of a variety of social cognitive skills which teach offenders to consider the consequences of their actions and develop a stronger repertoire of problem-solving techniques (see McGuire and Priestly, 1985 for examples).

An egocentric level of cognitive development has been linked not only with a deficit in moral reasoning but also with a lack of **empathy**, or an inability to sense another's feelings. Piaget suggested that small children are literally unable to take another's perspective, and that moving towards a position where this is possible is crucial in terms of more advanced cognitive understanding (moving from the pre-operational stage to the concrete operational stage). Taking someone else's perspective, however, is not simply a cognitive process since it also involves understanding and relating to their feelings. It is therefore suggested that continuing **egocentricism** may be linked to a failure to respect other people and develop empathy. Being able to imagine the distress of others can act as a brake on the behaviour most likely to cause this, so it is not surprising to discover that a lack of empathy is significantly associated with psychopathy (Blackburn, 1993). It has proved difficult to develop reliable measures of empathy, however, though findings which suggest that women are more empathic than men might present strategies for developing empathy in offenders, as well as explaining why less women are involved in crime. For instance, anger is said to disrupt empathy (Yates *et al.*, 1984) and if the display of aggression is an integral part of male socialisation then anger management training might be a useful first step towards developing empathy.

Uncontrolled episodes of anger may result from **impulsivity** or a tendency to follow impulses instinctively and without thought for the consequences. It has been suggested that this is a common characteristic of most offending behaviour, i.e. the satisfaction of immediate needs. Impulsivity is strongly associated with psychopathy and anti-social personality (Blackburn, 1993) and can be measured using the *Minnesota Multiphasic Inventory* (MMPI), though there are alternative measures which tap into an inability to defer gratification, or carelessness in performing motor tasks.

Another factor which is associated with criminality is an **external locus of control.** Rotter (1975) suggested that our beliefs about causality can be placed on a continuum whereby an external locus of control reflects a belief that outcomes are determined by external factors such as chance, situation or more powerful others. By contrast an **internal locus of control** reflects a belief that we can exert control over our destiny by exercising personal choices and actions. Offenders are said to differ from non-offenders in their tendency towards externality as a means of absolving themselves from responsibility.

Linked to locus of control explanations of crime is **attribution theory** which has become a central component of social cognition. We tend to explain our own and others' behaviour to ourselves by way of attributing motives. These are based on external factors but are often influenced by other factors too, such as prior assumptions. For instance, the way we assign blame and responsibility tends to be harsher in respect of others than in relation to ourselves. Thus hostile attributions may be made very quickly in a specific context like a pub or club and lead to aggression, while responsibility for this outcome is conveniently avoided by externally allocating intention. For example, I just pushed you because you deliberately knocked my drink (rather than it being an accident). Palmer and Hollin (2000) found that self-reported delinquency in young offenders was associated not only with lower levels of moral reasoning but also with increased tendencies to inaccurate attributions of hostility, especially in ambiguous situations where it may be difficult to accurately ascertain intentions.

• **Figure 2.1:** A hostile situation turns violent – a possible example of deindividuation (see p.5)

Theme link to Perspectives and Issues (**social psychology**)

Attribution theory focuses on the explanations we offer for our own and others' behaviour (Heider, 1958). The fundamental attribution error is our tendency to assign internal or dispositional factors in explaining others' behaviour while applying external or situational factors to our own (Ross, 1977). For example, if *you* slip on a banana skin it's because you're inherently clumsy, if *I* do it's because someone stupidly left a banana skin there for me to slip on.

Most of these cognitive explanations of crime assume that dysfunctional thought patterns produce inappropriate behaviour, and therefore by challenging these patterns and replacing them with more flexible thinking offending will be reduced. Cognitive restructuring now forms a major part of most contemporary treatment programmes.

Conclusions

So – after consideration of all these theories are we any wiser about the causes of crime? There are many types of crime, and many types of offender. Some experiences are shared, while others are very individual. Clearly we all have a genetic inheritance or genetic potential, but in order for that potential to be released there have to be some environmental triggers. It also seems clear that the roots of anti-social behaviour lie in early childhood, and that certain events in childhood can increase an individual's psychological vulnerability.

Factors in childhood which might increase vulnerability to criminality:

- insecure attachment
- a weak sense of self
- a dysfunctional family
- coercive or indifferent parenting
- physical, sexual, or emotional abuse, and/or neglect
- the death of a parent
- low family income
- an acrimonious separation or divorce
- low academic achievement.

However, these events can occur and be managed with sufficient sensitivity to ensure that children are not damaged by them. Therefore there is also a matching element between the child and its family environment, and a mismatch increases the child's vulnerability. Moreover, the dramatic rise in offending behaviour at adolescence and its subsequent decline in early adulthood suggests that social factors such as peer pressure, identity issues and alienation must be operating too.

Plomin (1994) has convincingly argued that genetics alone cannot explain adult behaviour, focusing on the way genes interact with the environment. He further suggests that the environment cannot be assumed as a constant, and that the *non-shared environment* is a crucial factor in determining adult outcomes for children in the same family. What seems to affect children most are the things they do not share with their siblings, the unique individual experiences which are often shared with their peers (Harris, 1998). Parents tend to think they raise their children in the same way, but families can alter over time, sometimes quite significantly, as a result of chronic illness, mental illness, unemployment, high mobility, or divorce. Children's own experiences will vary too, for example having an influential teacher, developing a new interest, gaining or losing a friend. Plomin suggests that it is these individual differences and the way they interact with our genetic make-up which produces personality differences.

Theme link to Perspectives and Issues (**individual differences**)

Vold *et al.* (1998) suggest that these individual differences are associated with an increased probability of committing crime, but the range indicates that we are still a long way from being able to offer a definitive explanation:

1. A history of early childhood problem behaviours and of being subjected to poor parental child-rearing techniques such as harsh and inconsistent discipline; school failure and the failure to learn higher cognitive skills such as moral reasoning, empathy, and problem-solving.

2. Certain neurotransmitter imbalances such as low serotonin, certain hormone imbalances such as high testosterone, central nervous system deficiencies such as frontal or temporal lobe dysfunction, and autonomic nervous system variations such as unusual reactions to anxiety.

3. Ingesting alcohol, many illegal drugs, and some toxins such as lead; head injuries, and pregnancy or birth complications.

4. Personality characteristics such as impulsivity, insensitivity, a physical and nonverbal orientation, and a tendency to take risks.

5. Thinking patterns that focus on trouble, toughness, smartness, excitement, fate and autonomy; an exaggerated sense of 'manliness'; a tendency to think in terms of short-term rather than long-term consequences; a tendency to see threats everywhere and to believe that it is appropriate to respond to threats with extreme violence.

6. Chronic physiological arousal and frequent experience of negative emotions, either because of an inability to escape from negative situations or because of a tendency to experience negative emotions in a wider range of situations than other people.

7. Association with others who are engaged in and approve of criminal behaviour.

8. Attachments to other people, less involvement in conventional activities, less to lose from committing crime, and weaker beliefs in the moral validity of the law.
(Vold *et al.*, p.323)

Identify the links with psychological concepts and research, and consider how these might be used to reduce the probability of offending in individuals or groups of individuals.

The emphasis on individual differences within psychology can provide a useful framework for recognising the diversity of crime and criminals, while also allowing a degree of targeting in relation to crime prevention strategies.

KEY TERMS

determinism versus free will
rational choice theory
cognitive dysfunction
social cognition
moral development
empathy
egocentricism
impulsivity
external locus of control
internal locus of control
attribution theory

EXERCISE 1

Think of crimes which have recently been reported in the newspapers. List the costs and benefits which offenders may have considered before they became involved in this range of crimes.

EXERCISE 2

How might you encourage moral development in young children? Construct some age-appropriate moral dilemmas for different groups of children, and ask them what they would do in such a situation. Compare the answers of boys and girls, and different age groups.

EXERCISE 3

Evaluate the role of free will in the onset of offending behaviour.

three

Crime–victim interaction

With all the emphasis on offenders – how best to catch them, why they committed their crimes, how they should be treated – victims often appear to be forgotten or marginalised in the process, and yet there are very few crimes without victims. Moreover, it is clear that some people are more likely to be the victims of crime than others. Farrell and Pease (1993) demonstrated that while 60% of the population do not experience crime in any one year, 40% suffer one or more crimes, and 4% of these victims suffer about 44% of all crimes. This chapter examines:

- who are the victims?
- fear of crime
- victim responses
- the nature of crime reporting.

Who are the victims of crime?

According to the 2000 British Crime Survey, the average chance of becoming a victim of violence in 1999 was 4.2%, though this risk varied according to gender and situation. For instance, young men aged 16–24 had a risk of violence factor of 20.1%, while men in general were the victims in 64% of muggings and 80% of stranger assaults. Domestic violence was the only category of violence where the risks for women were higher than for men. The risk of violence was higher in towns and cities too, with the risk in rural areas dropping to 2.7% from 4.2%. Personal factors which increased the risk of becoming a victim of violence included frequency of going out and living in rented accommodation, so for instance young male students living in inner cities who go out every weekend are likely to be in the highest risk group.

Becoming a victim of crime can in some cases be the most reliable indicator of whether that person is likely to become a victim again, particularly in relation to burglary (Pease, 1998). If burglars have found a house an easy target they may feel confident about breaking in again, they may tell criminal associates who then choose the same target, or they may return to take the items the householders have replaced on insurance (Ashton *et al.*, 1998). Measures can be taken to prevent recurrence, such as improving home security, and since most repeat offences are committed by chronic offenders, police targeting might result in the arrest of precisely those individuals from whom victims need protection (Pease, 1998). Repeat victimization also seems to be a feature of domestic violence and child abuse.

FEAR OF CRIME

Although it is difficult to accurately estimate the extent of crime, it is undoubtedly clear that people today are much more frightened of the possibility of becoming victims of crime than ever before. Interestingly, although violent crime only accounts for a small percentage of all offences, it is the fear of becoming a victim of violence which seems to determine most people's attitudes to crime, their behaviour, and their view of society. The 2000 British Crime Survey revealed that women were more worried than men about violent crime, with 25% of female respondents saying they were 'very worried' about being mugged or physically attacked by a stranger, and almost 3 in 10 of them 'very worried' about being raped. Black and Asian respondents were also far more worried about all types of crime than white respondents, with 41% of Asian and 37% of black respondents claiming they were 'very worried' about their home being burgled, compared to 18% of white respondents (Kershaw *et al.*, 2000).

• **Figure 3.1:** Sensationalist tabloid coverage of crime – does this increase fear of crime?

Ironically, those who are the least likely to become the victims of crime tend to be the most fearful. Thus, the elderly tend to be very fearful of 'street crime' such as robbery and assault and yet are the least likely victims of such crimes, while those who are most likely to be the victims of this type of attack, men aged 16–24 years, do not appear to be excessively worried. Goodey (1997) has argued that young men's apparent fearlessness is crucially tied to the constraints of masculinity which prevent them admitting their own vulnerability. Public perceptions of crime are often shaped by the media, with coverage of crime tending to focus on exceptional events such as sex and violence, which inevitably gives a skewed impression of levels of risk (Howitt, 1998). Vrij and Parker (1997) found that sensationalist coverage of crime (tabloids) produced higher levels of crime than did non-sensationalist coverage (broadsheets). Nevertheless, the fear of crime does have an impact on people's behaviour in that they may curtail their activities at certain times, or not attend particular events, and in so doing maintain their fear via the process of negative reinforcement. Another irony is that the home is not the safe haven it is often mistakenly believed to be, as the likelihood of victimization is higher from relatives, partners and close friends than from complete strangers.

CONSEQUENCES OF BECOMING A VICTIM OF CRIME

While irritation, inconvenience, and some anger may characterise the response of victims to minor crimes, it is clear that for more serious crimes the consequences for victims can be very severe. This is particularly so when an individual's safety and security has been threatened, leaving the victim feeling vulnerable and helpless. The growth of victim support schemes in the last few years has undoubtedly helped many victims of crime begin to come to terms with their trauma.

Factors which can affect the way people react to victims include their general view of the world and the control they believe they have over their own destiny. Psychologists can measure 'belief in a just world' and 'locus of control' and both of these concepts can influence people's ability to cope. While most of us are sympathetic towards victims of crime, there is often a self-preserving tendency to hold some victims more responsible for their fate than others. This is called a **belief in a just world**, because in order to preserve our sense of control we assume that the world is a fair place and that victims in some way 'get what they deserve', thus reducing our own fears of likely victimization (Lerner, 1970; Lupfer et al., 1998). Becoming a victim in these circumstances can cause acute distress. Individuals tend to have either an external or internal locus of control, the former believing that external factors shape the quality of their lives, while the latter believe that they can control what is happening to them (Rotter, 1966). Those with an external locus of control may be fatalistic about their chances of becoming a crime victim and therefore be less traumatised than someone who genuinely believes they took all reasonable precautions and consequently finds it difficult to come to terms with their misfortune and the blow to their belief system. Becoming a victim is a severe threat to an individual's sense of control and a sense of powerlessness can be difficult to overcome.

The American Psychological Association Task Force on the Victims of Crime and Violence listed the following as potential psychological consequences of being a victim: depression, anxiety, paranoia, loss of control, shame, embarrassment, vulnerability, helplessness, humiliation, anger, shock, feelings of inequity, increased awareness of mortality, tension, malaise, and fear (Kahn, 1984). Although the intensity of these symptoms will vary for individuals, and will undoubtedly be more severe for those who already suffer from mental health problems, it is clear that victimization can produce short-term and long-term consequences with which it can be very difficult to cope without professional help.

In cases of sexual assault the subsequent trauma experienced by victims may last several months and appears to follow a recognised pattern, not dissimilar to the experience of **post-traumatic stress disorder**. Resnick *et al.* (1993) report an initial reaction of shaking, trembling, confusion and restlessness which may last in an intense form for the first week following an assault, subside in the second, only to return in the third week. Victims may also experience depression, fatigue and problems with social adjustment. Although levels of anxiety and fear remain high, the other symptoms may begin to subside after two to three months. Psychological problems may continue for some individuals for many years following a sexual assault, often as a result of self-blame. This may be particularly acute in cases of acquaintance rape.

• **Figure 3.2:** Victim support worker explaining the scheme to a victim of crime

Victims of burglary or theft may also suffer acute distress, especially if the items stolen have personal significance and are impossible to replace. Those whose homes have been burgled may feel a sense of invasion and threat which is difficult to come to terms with. Their psychological and physical boundaries have been violated, and they may not feel at ease in their surroundings as a consequence. Unless police officers are trained to recognise this type of distress, their eagerness to obtain information about the crime may blind them to the reality of victimization. Those who suffer repeat victimization may have special counselling needs because of their loss of ability to protect themselves and their families (Shaw, 1999)

Crime reporting

The police routinely record and collate information on criminal offences committed in their area and submit an annual report to the Home Office. Comparisons can then be made between areas, in terms not only of criminal activity but also of clear-up rates.

While what constitutes crime is not always clear cut there is a need for pragmatism, and one way forward is to refer to offences which are reported to the police. These are publicly reported each year by the Home Office and often form the basis of criminological research. Unfortunately the data are not representative in any sense because we know that the vast majority of offences are not reported. This may be for a variety of reasons, for instance people may not always feel an offence is sufficiently serious to report to the police, or they may have little confidence that the police will be sympathetic or efficient in their response. Hollin (1992) estimates that only 25% of all crimes appear in the official statistics, leaving a 'dark figure' of unreported crime inaccessible to researchers, while Coleman and Moynihan (1996) describe criminologists as ghostbusters in search of the elusive 'dark figure of crime'.

What do the **official crime statistics** tell us? Basically they tell us how many offences across a range of categories have been notified to the police over the previous twelve months. Between 2000 and 2001 just over five million crimes were recorded, and between the 1970s and the 1990s there was an average annual increase of about 5%. The belief that crime has increased is undoubtedly borne out by the official crime statistics, for instance in 1950 there were 500,000 reported crimes, and in 1970 1.6 million. During the 1990s however, overall recorded crime appeared to fall, although violent and sexual crimes increased (Povey, Cotton and Sisson, 2001).

TOTAL RECORDED CRIME BY OFFENCE 2000–01, ENGLAND AND WALES						
					Number of offences and percentages	
Offence group	12 months ending		Change			
	March 2000	March 2001	Number		Percentage	
Violence against the person	581,036	600,873	19,837	(78,248)	3.4	(15.6)
Sexual offences	37,792	37,299	−493	(1,618)	−1.3	(4.5)
Robbery	84,277	95,154	10,877	(17,442)	12.9	(26.1)
Total violent crime	**703,105**	**733,326**	**30,221**	**(97,308)**	**4.3**	**(16.1)**
Burglary	906,468	836,027	−70,441	(−46,716)	−7.8	(−4.9)
Total theft & handling stolen goods	2,223,620	2,145,372	−78,248	(32,181)	3.5	(1.5)
Theft of and from vehicles	**1,043,918**	**968,447**	**−75,471**	**(−33,808)**	**−7.2**	**(−3.1)**
Fraud & forgery	334,773	319,324	−15,449	(55,270)	−4.6	(19.8)
Criminal damage	945,682	960,087	14,405	(66,096)	1.5	(7.5)
Total property crime	**4,410,543**	**4,260,810**	**−149,733**	**(106,831)**	**−3.4**	**(2.5)**
Drug offences	121,866	113,458	−8,408	(−14,079)	−6.9	(−10.4)
Other notifiable offences	65,671	63,237	−2,434	(−2,036)	−3.7	(3.2)
Total all offences	**5,301,185**	**5,170,831**	**−130,354**	**(192,096)**	**−2.5**	**(3.8)**
Changes between 1998/99 and 1999/00 in brackets.						

Partly as a response to criticisms of the official crime statistics, the Home Office developed an alternative source of data – the British Crime Survey (BCS). This was first conducted in 1982, and every two years thereafter, though from 2001 it will be an annual collection of responses from a large sample of the public. Interviews are conducted asking people about the crimes committed against them during a given period. The results are not directly comparable with the official statistics, because different offence categories are used, but an alternative picture of crime is provided which many people believe is a more accurate account. There are 4.5 times as many crimes occurring according to the British Crime Survey than the police record, and victimization is unequally distributed amongst the population. The BCS 2000 reported a 4% drop in violent crimes but a rise of 29% in stranger violence – over half of which involved offenders who had been drinking, and the victims were almost all men. The most likely victims of crime were again identifed as men aged 16–24, while other high-risk groups were single parents, the unemployed, private renters, and women aged 16–24. Public pessimism about the problem of crime remained high, with two-thirds of respondents believing that crime had risen between 1997 and 1999, and 6% of respondents claiming that fear of crime greatly affected their quality of life.

The 2000 International Crime Victimization survey compares the experience of crime victims across seventeen countries. It confirms that since the mid-1990s the crime rate across the world has fallen, but unlike America, crime levels in England and Wales are still higher than they were at the end of the 1980s. Moreover, England and Wales are top of the league for car theft, with 2.6% of all car owners suffering the loss of their vehicle in the previous twelve months, and second only to Australia for high rates of burglary, assault and sexual assault. This discrepancy between politicians' claims that their policies have resulted in a drop in the official crime rate and the responses of crime victims highlights the need for a meaningful strategy for crime prevention which is not simply related to winning votes.

Media coverage of crime often perpetuates the myth that criminals are different from the rest of us, which can be a reassuring delusion because it suggests that we ought to be able to tell when we are interacting with a criminal. The reality is that differences between offenders and non-offenders are often minimal, and most self-report surveys carried out with non-offenders reveal that the majority of young males engage in some criminal activity during adolescence (for example Furnham and Thompson, 1991).

Summary

Measuring crime accurately is not easy, and in order to improve the effectiveness of our response we need not only official presentations of crime statistics but also the data from victim surveys. What has been learned is that the best predictor of victimization is previous experience of being a victim, and therefore this must inform police planning and crime prevention strategies. Fear of crime can seriously affect the quality of people's lives and yet often their anxiety is based on unrepresentative and inaccurate accounts of crime in the media. Nonetheless, becoming a crime victim is likely to provoke unexpectedly serious psychological symptoms which can benefit from appropriate counselling.

KEY TERMS

fear of crime
British Crime Survey
repeat victimization
belief in a just world
post-traumatic stress disorder
official crime statistics

Look through a daily newspaper for accounts of particular crimes. What factors are stressed, and what implicit or explicit suggestions are made as to why certain individuals acted in the way they did? How convincing are the explanations, and what real evidence is there to support them? Are any moral judgements made in relation to particular types of crime?

Identify some newspaper accounts of the same crime in tabloid newspapers and broadsheets. How are the stories presented differently? Look at the headline, the vocabulary used, and the photos. To what extent are different audiences being catered for? Show the tabloid and broadsheet versions to two different groups of participants, and then ask them about their fear of crime by presenting them with statements you can measure on a Likert scale. See Vrij and Parker (1997) who found that exposure to tabloid coverage of crime increased fear of crime.

Answer these questions in small groups but don't look at the answers until you have attempted all of the questions.

1. Have crime rates risen or fallen in the last ten years?
2. What proportion of crimes involve violence?
3. Is the UK murder rate rising or falling?
4. Are more or less offenders imprisoned compared to five years ago?
5. Is the rate of child abduction and murder going up?
6. Are women more likely to be attacked than men?
7. Are old people right to be so afraid of crime?
8. What percentage of men in the UK have a criminal record by the age of forty?
9. Which age group is most at risk of becoming a murder victim?

1. Recorded crime has fallen in recent years (14% between 1995 and 1997).
2. Only 6% of crimes are violent or sexual.
3. The UK murder rate is going down. There were 681 murders in 1996, 10% fewer than in 1995.
4. There are more offenders imprisoned now than five years ago (44,000 to 66,000).
5. The rate is unchanged over the last twenty years – about 7 children a year are murdered by a stranger. The real risk is in families, where 60–70 children are killed each year by their parents.
6. Women are three times less likely to be attacked than men.
7. The elderly are less at risk from violent crime than the young. Those aged under 29 are thirteen times more likely to be attacked than a pensioner.
8. 31.5% of British men have a criminal record for a non-motoring offence by the time they reach the age of 30.
9. Children under the age of twelve months (57 in every million).

four

Offender profiling

Identifying patterns of criminal activity has been a major concern of the police in terms of using their resources effectively and preventing crime, but attaching meaning to those patterns has tended to lack focus. Psychologists have been able to assist the police in this area by offering advice on the likely background of offenders based on their offence behaviour. They have also been able to advise on the analysis of statistical crime data in order to identify particular crime patterns such as repeat victimization. It is against this background of productive liaison between the police and psychologists that **offender profiling** has developed. In this chapter we will examine:

- definitions, approaches and developing a profile
- biases and pitfalls in profiling
- applied profiling.

In spite of all the popular fictional accounts of the technique and successes of offender profiling, the viability of the process itself remains unproven. Discussion of its efficacy is contentious, with one of the UK's most renowned practitioners of **investigative psychology**, David Canter, remarking that offender profiles are, 'often little more than, at best, subjective opinion, common sense, or ignorance, or at worst deliberate deception' (Canter and Alison, p.6) and that 'much of what passes for offender profiling (both) in practice and as reported in the factual and fictional media has no basis in empirical research'. (Canter, p.23)

Even Hannibal Lecter offers to construct a psychological profile for FBI agent Clarice Starling in *The Silence of the Lambs* while suggesting that psychology is not a credible science in *Hannibal*! Although productive work between psychologists and the police in relation to crime investigation will surely increase, the significant progress which has been made in relation to DNA (deoxyribonucleic acid) analysis may diminish the contribution of profiling while simultaneously raising concerns about possible civil liberties violations.

There are a range of definitions of profiling and Gudjonsson and Copson (1997) suggest this is because:

> Profiling is neither a readily identifiable nor a homogenous entity and its status is properly regarded as a professional sideline not amounting to a true science … Little has been published to shed light on what profilers actually do or how they do it. (1997 p.76)

This is clearly not for want of trying, given the number of fictional accounts of profiling, but even practitioners remain divided about profiling, with conflicting views about both theory and methodology. Put simply, psychological offender profiling is an attempt to produce a description or profile of an offender by analysing the characteristics of the offence and other background information. Investigators analyse the crime scene in order to infer personality traits from the way the offender acted before, during and after the offence. This information is then compared to a database of characteristics of previous offenders and offence patterns in an attempt to develop a working profile which can inform the investigation. The overall aim of profiling is to move from data to inference and construct a behavioural composite which will then enable the police to evaluate their list of suspects, matching information from the crime scene with suspect characteristics.

Offender profiling is not appropriate for all criminal offences, but for certain categories it can be useful. These include arson, serial rape and murder. The police normally only call in a profiler if a serious crime has occurred and there are few clues with no obvious suspects. This is often because the public alarm about these types of offence creates a need for a visible and rapid response, but also because it is these offences which are most likely to reveal psychological evidence about the offender. The production of a profile should never be regarded as evidential in terms of targeting a particular suspect or there may be a danger of self-fulfilling prophecies and a very weak prosecution case.

How did profiling develop?

Attempting to match psychological or physical qualities to particular types of crime has a long literary history, but criminal or offender profiling as we now know it began in 1943 when the US Office of Strategic Services asked a psychiatrist, Walter Langer, to draw up a profile of Adolf Hitler. Langer (1972) compiled a psychodynamic personality profile of Hitler which took considerable account of his parents' influence on him, especially his mother. Langer suggested that Hitler's mother's death from cancer had affected her son at a critical time, and this had resulted in an inability to sustain intimate relationships, a belief in his own infallibility, and a determination to prove his masculinity. The profile was requested so that an interrogation strategy could be developed should Hitler ever be captured. In fact, Langer pointed out that if capture was imminent Hitler would commit suicide, which he did in 1945.

After the war, Lionel Haward, a psychologist working for the Royal Air Force, drew up a list of characteristics which high-ranking Nazi war criminals might display if captured. Then in 1956, James Brussel, an American psychiatrist, drew up what turned out to be an uncannily accurate profile of a bomber who had been terrorising New York for several years. In fact Brussel (1968) relied heavily on his prior knowledge of psychopathology, common sense, and revealing evidence left at the crime scenes, all of which contributed to the eventual arrest of George Metesky and the astonishment of the press (see box below). Significantly Metesky was identified not because of the profile, but because of information in the personnel files of the company against which he held a grudge. Nonetheless, Brussel's description of Metesky was very accurate and is probably the first well-publicised example of the potential of profiling.

The mad bomber of New York

James Brussel predicted that the suspect would be:

- a male high school graduate, aged 40–50 years
- living in Connecticut or Westchester, probably with a sister or maiden aunt
- Slavic and Catholic
- likely to wear a buttoned-up double-breasted suit.

When George Metesky was arrested he turned out to be 54, Polish, living in Connecticut with two older sisters, and wearing a double-breasted suit, but Brussel already knew that:

- bombing is a crime associated with paranoid personality disorders which tend to peak around the age of 40 years
- bombs at that time tended to be a middle European protest strategy
- errors in the letters indicated non-US origins
- most middle Europeans are Catholics, and in New York tend to concentrate in either Connecticut or Westchester, where there are strong family ties
- the bombing style was meticulous, suggesting someone for whom order was important, and this could translate into the dress sense of the day
- there was evidence in the letters from the bomber that he believed he had been treated badly by his employers, Consolidated Edison.

In 1978 the FBI established a psychological profiling programme within their Behavioural Support Unit, to be followed by the National Center for the Analysis of Violent Crime in 1984. Data produced from these groups related to criminal investigations together with interview information from incarcerated offenders, child molestors and serial murderers. The aim was to identify the major personality characteristics of serious offenders and how they differed from non-offenders, and led FBI officers to propose theoretical frameworks for distinguishing between types of offender, for instance between 'organised' and 'disorganised' offences and offenders (Ressler *et al.*, 1988). Some offences were carried out after considerable forward planning and an element of victim targeting, while others appeared to be committed impulsively with victims chosen at random. It was suggested that the crime scenes revealed clear evidence of whether offences had been committed by 'organised' or 'disorganised' offenders (see box below). Informed analysis of the crime scene could then be used to draw up a profile which would help the police to narrow their pool of suspects and focus their investigation.

FBI crime scene analysis

Organised	Disorganised
evidence of planning	spontaneous offence
victim targeted	victim or location known
victim personalised	victim depersonalised
controlled conversation	minimal conversation
crime scene reflects control	crime scene random or sloppy
victim submissive	sudden violence to victim
use of restraints	minimal use of restraints
aggressive acts prior to death	sexual acts after death
body hidden	body left in view
weapon and evidence absent	weapon and evidence often present

Using this type of classification system was also considered crucial for determining whether the same person had committed a series of offences if there were similar features at each crime scene. The Crime Classification Manual (Ressler *et al.*, 1992) was subsequently developed to assist investigators in identifying whether a series of offences was committed by the same offender, and estimating the likelihood of a repeat offence and escalation of violence.

It is the FBI's approach to offender profiling which seems to have captured the public imagination, though on methodological grounds it has been consistently criticised – not only is it based on a very small sample of cases, but it has been subject to very little formal scientific evaluation, and appears to be based on subjective interpretation (Oleson, 1996, Canter, 1994). The sample of interviewees were all convicted so might not have been representative of the entire population of serial murderers, or indeed serial murderers in countries other than America. Rossmo (1996) goes so far as to suggest that the FBI methodology is lacking in 'programme validity and reliability research (and lacks) a proper theoretical basis', while Canter and Alison (1999) state that:

> a careful examination of the content of their profiles reveals a severe lack in the accounts of any systematic procedures or any substantive, theoretical models of behaviour. There is no reference to any commonly accepted psychological principles – pathological or social.

Reliance on the classification system is also criticised because it carries with it the assumption that offenders have a consistent pattern of motivation which does not change. Despite these criticisms, the FBI model has influenced the development of profiling in most countries, and in America the vast majority of profilers are not forensic psychologists but have advanced through the ranks of the FBI.

The value of setting up a database with details of previous offending was recognised in the UK following the official inquiry into the shortfalls of the Yorkshire Ripper investigation, where the sheer volume of collected evidence overwhelmed the police team and hindered the effectiveness of the operation. In 1986 the CATCHEM database was established with the aim of collecting all known data on child murders in the UK since 1960. This database has proved invaluable for police investigations of child abductions since common elements have been identified which can then guide police in the most effective use of their resources during a critical period. For instance, 96% of children who go missing are dead within twenty-four hours, and in the vast majority of cases the perpetrator is known to the victim. The CATCHEM database can also generate a list of possible offender characteristics from details of an offence, which will narrow down the police investigation.

In the UK the potential of offender profiling was recognised as a result of the work of David Canter (1994), and his involvement in the case of John Duffy (the Railway Rapist) who was convicted in 1988 for two murders and five

• **Figure 4.1:** John Duffy, the Railway Rapist

David Canter's profile of John Duffy

Profile of likely offender	Match
live in the Kilburn or Cricklewood area of London, the area where the first three offences occurred	Duffy lived in Kilburn
be married, with no children	Duffy was married, and a low sperm count meant he was infertile
have marriage problems	Duffy and his wife were separated
be a loner, with few friends	Duffy had only two male friends, one of whom was David Mulcahy, his co-offender
be physically small, with feelings of unattractiveness	Duffy was 5′4″, with acne
have an interest in martial arts or body building	Duffy spent much of his time at a martial arts club
need to dominate women	Duffy was a violent man who had already attacked his wife
have fantasies about rape and bondage	Duffy liked tying up his wife before sex

have a fascination for weapons, especially swords and knives	Duffy had many 'Kung Fu' style weapons in his home
have fantasies about sex and violence	Duffy collected hard-core porn videos
keep souvenirs from crimes	Duffy had 33 door keys, each taken from a victim as a souvenir
hold a semi-skilled job with little contact with the public	Duffy trained as a carpenter with British Rail
be in the age range 20–30	Duffy was 28 when arrested, and had been a rapist for 4 years

rapes. This case highlights the creative tension between psychological profiling and the realities of criminal investigation, legal constraints, and scientific advances. Duffy was originally 1505th in a list of 2000 suspects but Canter's profile, developed from analysis of the crime scenes and victim statements, enabled a prompt police response. At the time of Duffy's conviction the police knew that he had not been offending alone and suspected his childhood friend, David Mulcahy, but they could not produce enough evidence to link him with the offences because DNA profiling was not sufficiently developed. However, 13 years later in 2001, Mulcahy was sentenced to life imprisonment for his involvement in the rapes and murders, on the basis of testimony provided by Duffy after counselling sessions with a prison psychologist, sophisticated DNA evidence derived from samples kept from the original offences, and determined police investigation.

Canter subsequently developed his own system of crime analysis based firmly on psychological principles and with both theoretical and methodological rigour. He calls his approach 'investigative psychology' to distinguish it from the FBI methods, which he regards as largely subjective and intuitive and therefore completely at odds with a scientific tradition of empirical investigation. What is required instead are:

> explanatory frameworks that can lead to hypotheses about the sort of offender characteristics that are likely to relate to particular offence behaviour. (Canter, 2000, p.27)

The emphasis on *behaviour* is important since the value of offender profiling can only be in terms of its practical use to investigating authorities. Hence, speculation about offender motivation is meaningless unless it impacts directly on prevention and detection. Canter has developed a range of methodologies including Facet Theory, Small Space Analysis, and Multi-dimensional Scaling to investigate offence patterns and develop models for differentiating between offender types. Details of these statistical approaches to profiling have been placed in the public domain for other researchers to evaluate and develop, in marked contrast to the work of the FBI.

Canter's approach is rooted in both social and environmental psychology. He believes that offenders, like all other people, act consistently, in that their actions have some internal coherence whatever the setting. An analysis of their behaviour during the commission of an offence – regarded as a social interaction – will reveal a pattern which offers clues to their lifestyle during the non-offending parts of their life. Thus, he says:

> What does a criminal reveal about himself by the way he commits a crime? … as well as … material traces he also leaves psychological traces, tell-tale patterns of behaviour that indicate the sort of person he is. Gleaned from the crime scene and reports from witnesses, these traces are more ambiguous and subtle than those examined by the biologist or physicist … They are more like shadows [which] … can indicate where investigators should look and what sort of person they should be looking for. (Canter, 1994, p.4)

Canter believes that the way an offender behaves during a crime mirrors the way he behaves in his everyday life, since the way we conduct all our interactions is ingrained and quite difficult to disguise convincingly. Thus the interaction between the offender and his victim reveals clues from which an investigator can draw inferences. This may be particularly evident in the speech style chosen by the offender, while even the choice of victim is highly signficant in the context of the offender's life.

Theme link to Perspectives and Issues
(cognitive psychology and schema theory)

Additionally Canter introduces the concept of **mental maps** as a way of interpreting the geographical pattern of offending. Each of us has a different cognitive schema to help us understand where we live. This is affected by the emphasis we might place on particular areas, or the routes we normally take to school or work, so they are not literal maps. Offenders have their own mental maps too, and when they commit offences they tend to keep within certain boundaries, mainly because they have more knowledge of certain areas and will be able to look inconspicuous. Their pattern of offending can be quite revealing, and geographical mapping together with crime pattern analysis have considerable potential for police investigations.

Geographic profiling of crime may appear to be a recent development, but analysing the geography of crime is not new. Its emphasis is away from the individual characteristics and personality of the offender, and more towards the recording of offences and likely offender residences or workplaces. Perhaps the most well known attempt to pinpoint a geographical pattern of offending was that of the Chicago School. Criminologists Shaw and McKay (1942) analysed the pattern of juvenile delinquency in Chicago, and were able to identify zones of the city which were particularly crime-prone. These zones were characterised by rapidly changing populations, low rents, deprivation, and ineffective socialisation of children. Shaw and McKay subsequently developed their social disorganisation theory of crime suggesting that delinquency was likely to become the norm in such areas, with offending behaviour readily transmitted via gang culture.

Technological developments have produced much more sophisticated techniques for mapping crime, most notably Geographic Information Systems or GIS and Criminal Geographic Targeting or CGT, and the potential for these techniques in terms of crime prevention is significant. However, the effectiveness of geographic profiling is very much dependent on the accuracy of the data collected by the police. Rossmo (1997) suggests that geographic profiling of serial offences can provide information about the possible relationship between crime and place which then helps to identify the offender's home. More practical applications of geographic profiling might enable the police to use their resources more effectively. For instance if homes in a particular area tend to be burgled at a particular time of day, this might be explained by the finishing times at the local comprehensive school. An appropriate response would be more patrols in the area at that time, together with some community police initiatives in liaison with the school.

There is also the clinical approach to profiling, exemplified by forensic psychiatrists such as Richard Badcock (1997). Their practitioner experience with disturbed offenders leads them to focus on developmental life events which may have shaped the offender's personality and are subsequently revealed in offending patterns. For instance, an individual who has experienced abuse as a child may experience problems in forming normal relationships as an adult. If the legacy of abuse has not been resolved there may be a reservoir of frustration, anger and envy which is released through a particular type of offending, characterised by the exercise of control and power, or an excessive use of violence. Another approach based on clinical experience focuses on links between types of offending behaviour and particular mental states, such as psychoses and personality disorders.

HOW IS A PROFILE DEVELOPED?

Holmes and Holmes (1996) suggest that profiling has three major goals which will influence how a profile is developed, namely:

a)   a social and psychological assessment of the offender

b)   a psychological evaluation of possessions found with suspected offenders

c)   consultation with law enforcement officials on the strategies which might best be employed when interviewing suspects.
     (1996 p.156)

while Dale (1997) suggests that asking key questions should produce the information required, for instance:

analysis of how, where, when and to whom crime is occurring should allow research to be conducted which would lead to a greater understanding of why crime is occurring and, to a degree, the type of person committing it. (1997 p.105)

Forensic scientists and Scene of Crime Officers (SOCOs) will already have collected physical evidence from the crime scene, and psychologists will then examine the scene for clues which might give indicators of the offender's personality characteristics. They will also analyse victim statements and the pattern of offending, if there have been repeat offences of a similar nature. Some of the questions which may be asked include:

the offence

What was the nature of the crime? Clearly murder is at the top of the scale, but there may be other elements of the crime which are significant in terms of providing information about the offender, For example was the victim held in captivity and tortured, were victims alone or were there sometimes multiple victims, was there one offender or several, were there elements of sexual sadism, or a degree of planning, suggesting obsession and possible prior stalking behaviour? The more complex the crime the more intelligent the offender is likely to be, which will have implications for interrogation.

timing of offences

What is the time period between offences, and does it have significance, for example an absence of offending while a suspected offender was in prison, working abroad, or in hospital? Is the time of offending significant in terms of employment pattern, e.g. shift-work, and is the time period between offences changing, suggesting either caution or increased appetite?

offending site

Where was the offence carried out? Offenders may have a location which is isolated and stocked with all the items they will need, or they may use their own home. Alternatively they may choose offending sites like the victims' homes, carparks or recreation areas. Their crime site may be chosen on the basis of opportunism or precise targeting, for instance victims living alone. The majority of offenders tend to offend within a small radius of their home, although there are 'commuters' who are prepared to travel long distances to commit their offences.

body deposition site

If a victim has been killed, why did the offender choose to leave the body in a particular location? Was keeping the body hidden or making its location blatanty obvious the motivation for choice of dump site? Kenneth Bianchi and Angelo Buono displayed the naked bodies of some of their victims where all of Hollywood could see them, almost as if to taunt the authorities. Some offenders, for instance Peter Sutcliffe, have returned to dump sites and moved the position of the bodies to ensure that they are found more easily, suggesting that the response of the police and the media is almost as important as the offence itself.

pattern of injuries

Is there any significance in the pattern of injuries on the victims, for example, ligature marks, defence injuries, wounds inflicted on particular parts of the body, types of weapon used, injuries inflicted clinically or in anger? What was the extent of force used? The injuries will not only yield forensic evidence but an indication of what went on between offender and victim – was the victim conscious, how were they subdued, was bondage a signficant part of the offending behaviour or a means to the end? The type of weapon used indicates the degree of premediation, for instance whether a murder tool kit was brought to the scene, or weapons were used impulsively because they were to hand. The blood pattern may reveal whether the offender was right or left handed.

signature

The offender may leave an indicator that he alone was the offender, a particular pattern of injuries or a display at the crime scene which the investigating team will recognise, e.g. the use of a special garotte. This indicates narcissism, pride in his work, and taunting the investigators. The signature may be part of an offender's ritualistic fantasy which has to be compulsively repeated, but it can yield important information. Douglas and Olshaker (1995) suggest that an offender's signature does not alter, even though the modus operandi may change.

capture style

How did the victim end up with the offender? Were they fooled into thinking there was no danger, e.g. the offender posed as an authority figure, or knew some information from prior stalking which was used to persuade the victim they could trust the offender. Witnesses may be able to supply information about the capture style, but other factors may be indicative – for instance, Fred and Rosemary West were able to persuade some of their victims to get into their car at bus-stops because they offered them a lift, and appeared to pose no threat as they seemed to be a normal married couple. Similarly, Ted Bundy pretended to have his arm in a sling in order to persuade some of his victims to help him move things out of his vehicle before he bundled them into the car. Other offenders may be ruthlessly efficient in terms of capture, suggesting some prior experience or training, possibly in the armed forces.

interaction style

The interaction between offender and victim may be brief or unbearably long, but it will provide crucial evidence about the offender, his usual social pattern of interaction, his attitude to women, his accent, clues about his employment and lifestyle, the element of offence planning, etc. This evidence will only be available if the victims survive. The behavioural scripting can be part of the offender's ritual, for instance telling the victim not to look at their face, or forcing them to pretend they are consenting. How the victim's clothes were removed can also be significant, for instance whether they were ripped off or the victim was made to remove their own clothes. The interaction style will be revealed in the offending pattern, for instance whether the offender views his victims as objects or people, whether a pseudo relationship is important, or anonymity and silence are essential. Covering the victim's face may indicate an unwillingness to engage with the reality of the offence, a complete lack of empathy, a desire not to be recognised, or part of a sexual fantasy.

sex

Is there any significance in the sexual acts performed, evidence of sexual dysfunction (premature or retarded ejaculation, impotence) or paraphilias (fetishism, paedophilia, necrophilia, sadism)? Evidence of bondage may reveal the offender was simply trying to restrain the offender, or there may be a sexual significance if there are unnecessary bindings or a symmetry to the ligatures.

pattern of victims/victimology

Why did the offender choose this person as a victim? Was the victim known? To answer these questions the investigator needs to compile a complete history of the victim – their age, gender, race, lifestyle, personality traits, appearance, reputation, social network, routines, financial circumstances, alcohol or drug abuse. This may provide clues which relate the offender to the victim, and may also inform future victim selection and effective interrogation strategies. Selection of elderly victims by a young offender with a sexual motive suggests a chronic condition known as gerontophilia, while evidence of stalking prior to victim contact may suggest obsessional erotomania. Pathological states suggest a range of other identifiable characteristics associated with the condition.

Ted Bundy chose as victims women who looked like the girl who had once rejected him – their hairstyles were all very similar, and they appeared to be intelligent and middle-class. Harold Shipman's choice of sick elderly women as victims was said to symbolically represent his unresolved grief at losing his own mother to cancer, though more pragmatically his victims were also compliant, already ill, and their deaths were unlikely to arouse suspicion. Jeffrey Dahmer said he chose his victims on the basis of their looks, but they were also often in a category where they were unlikely to be missed. Similarly, Frederick and Rosemary West chose their vulnerable female victims on the basis of opportunism, together with low chances of their disappearances being seriously followed up.

trophies/souvenirs

These can be items removed from the victim, or photos and videos taken at the crime scene. This allows the offender to relive the experience of committing the offence. John Duffy took door keys from his victims, while Paul Bernardo took videos of his offences and catalogued them in his home.

• **Figure 4.2:** Artist's impression of Manchester doctor Harold Shipman in the dock at Preston Crown Court, Jan 31, 2000. He was convicted of murdering 15 of his female patients and is now Britain's most prolific serial killer

Offenders may also keep a journal or diary about their offending, and this seems an important element of the offending pattern and also indicates a sense of invulnerability to detection.

previous history

There will probably be a history of minor offending (indecent exposure, voyeurism, nuisance calls, theft or burglary), and an escalation of violence during the signficant period of offending. Offenders' fantasies may also have been acted out in their previous relationships, for example wearing uniforms, asking their partners to participate in bondage or dress like children. To some extent this is a form of rehearsal before the first offence.

A complete absence of forensic evidence may indicate that the offender has previous forensic awareness, either from prior offending, or because he is familiar with the criminal justice system. Using rubber gloves or forcing the victim to bathe in order to remove forensic evidence suggests a degree of sophistication and forensic awareness.

EVALUATION OF PROFILING

Campbell (1976) suggested ominously that 'there is no clear evidence that psychologists are any better than bartenders at the remote diagnosis of killers' (p.119) and 22 years later Canter and Alison (1999) suggested that in many accounts of profiling 'systematic observations or procedures are discouraged in favour of instinct and intuition' (p.7). Their view is that profiling as it is popularly described is insufficiently grounded in psychological principles of empirical investigation, and does not always adhere to the ethical framework required by the British Psychological Society.

O'Keefe and Alison (2001) suggest that profiling may suffer from a possible Barnum effect whereby people, in this case police officers, are presented with ambiguous, generalised statements and then see what they want to see in the content, disregarding what does not fit in with their overall perspective. When there is considerable pressure on police officers to make an arrest, they may seize upon statements made by profilers as a result of the pressure rather than the convincing nature of the profile. Within this context profilers are seen by some to operate in much the same way as astrologers and **psychic detectives** who have previously assisted the police. O'Keefe and Alison found in their study that psychic detectives were in fact no more accurate in their predictions than controls, and relied on a variety of rhetorical devices associated with the cold reading strategies used by psychics in telling people's fortunes.

Pinizzotto and Finkel (1990) attempted to discover whether professional profilers would be more accurate than informed laypersons in drawing up profiles from two closed police cases, and so they compared groups of profilers, detectives, psychologists, and students. What they found was that the profilers did indeed produce richer and more detailed profiles, and that they correctly predicted the characteristics of the convicted offenders. Pinizzotto and Finkel concluded that this was the result of their confidence and experience rather than an exclusive technique. When Kocsis *et al.* (2000) repeated this paradigm, however, including a group of self-declared psychics, the professional profilers demonstrated a superior set of skills for the task, while the psychics seemed to rely on little more than social stereotypes. Significantly the performance of the group of psychologists was better than that of the other non-profiler groups, suggesting that some psychological knowledge is of benefit to the process of profiling.

HOW SUCCESSFUL IS PROFILING?

The extent to which profiling has been successful is difficult to estimate since the successes are given considerable media attention, while the failures are not. A notable exception was the Rachel Nickell murder investigation in 1994 which led to the very public dismissal of the case against Colin Stagg, because of the involvement of profiler Paul Britton. Britton had worked with the police in trying to get a confession from Stagg, using a covert operation involving a female police officer posing as a girlfriend interested in violence. The attempt was unsuccessful and the judge was very critical of the legal and ethical flaws in such an operation.

Even estimating profiling's contribution to success within a complex police operation is problematic, and it is clear that there are some tensions and misunderstandings between profilers and the police (Copson, 1995; Oleson, 1996). Copson and Holloway (1997) suggest that profiling led to the identification of an offender in less than 3% of the 184 cases they studied, and this may be where part of the problem in evaluation lies. There is often an imperative to identify a suspect as soon as possible, and profiling alone cannot provide this kind of service. As Jackson and Bekarian (1997) note:

> ... the answers that are offered are not solutions. Offender profiles do not solve crimes. Instead ... profiles should be viewed as simply one more tool that can be extremely useful in guiding strategy development, supporting information management, and improving case understanding. (1997 p.3)

Summary

Applying psychological principles to the investigation of crime has obvious potential but it must be managed appropriately within an ethical and regulatory framework. Analysis informed by theoretical knowledge grounded in empirical research can help the police focus their energies and target their resources. If offender profiling and crime analysis are going to develop this potential, however, then appropriate publication and evaluation of the techniques is required, together with a productive and realistic working relationship between the police and forensic psychologists.

KEY TERMS

offender profiling
investigative psychology
organised/disorganised typology
mental maps
crime scene analysis
geographic profiling
psychic detectives

EXERCISE 1

(a) Consider and evaluate psychological studies of offender profiling
(b) Suggest what the aims of offender profiling should be, and provide reasons for your answer

EXERCISE 2

What characteristics, experience and qualifications do you think an offender profiler should possess?

EXERCISE 3

Is offender profiling sufficiently scientific?

The police and crime

The relationship between the police and academics has often been a delicate one, with the legacy of accusations of racism, sexual harassment and brutality, encapsulated in the concept of **police canteen culture**, remaining as a barrier to productive liaison (Mitchell and Munroe, 1996). During the 1960s, when labelling theory was popular, it was suggested that police bias and reliance on stereotypes resulted in the production and amplification of deviance (Piliavin and Briar, 1964). Certainly a view of police officers developed which portrayed them as suspicious, cynical and likely to close ranks if criticised (Graef, 1990). Within this context it is perhaps not surprising that the police were suspicious of offers of help from outsiders such as academic psychologists. However, with the development of community policing in the 1980s and an acknowledgement of the need to tackle crime from a multi-agency perspective, the potential of interdependent working between police, sociologists and psychologists was recognised and encouraged.

In America and the UK a series of incidents highlighted the need for police officers to receive stress counselling after traumatic events, and also social skills training to manage public disorder. They also alerted police authorities to the usefulness of developing support services, using the expertise of clinical and occupational psychologists. There then followed appointments of research staff who could collaborate with academic psychologists in evaluating particular police procedures and experiences (see Brown, 1998).

Psychology now forms an essential part of police training, though it is often taught by police officers. Psychological concepts and methodologies have become an accepted part of a range of police activities, including selection and recruitment, interviewing suspects and victims, crime analysis, developing and evaluating crime-reduction strategies. A psychology degree is now seen as beneficial for police officers, and individual officers can be seconded onto postgraduate psychology courses. This is not to deny that a certain resistance to contributions from psychologists still exists, however, and police culture is notoriously insular. This is confirmed by recent admissions that institutionalised racism continues to exist within the police despite considerable efforts to address the problem.

Recruitment and selection

Since many criticisms levelled at police practice are aimed not only at the organisation but also at individuals, selection of the 'right' sort of police recruit becomes essential. Gone are the days when to become a police officer all a candidate needed was to be over a certain height and have good character references. Educational qualifications are now seen as important, as are specific attitudes, aptitude, skills and abilities. Indeed one of the earliest contributions by psychologists to the American police involved the use of standard IQ tests in the selection process, with a score of 80 set as the minimum standard (Reese, 1995). Psychologists have subsequently developed a wide range of **psychometric tests** to measure appropriate characteristics, and many organisations have used test batteries successfully in recruitment, though these have not always proved entirely suitable for police selection procedures (Gowan and Gatewood 1995).

• **Figure 5.1:** Police recruits in Hendon

Is there a **police personality?** Is the development of a police personality the result of the context in which police officers work rather than their individual characteristics? This is the classic person – situation debate within social psychology.

There is a popular belief that particular personality types are attracted to police work. Siegal (1986) suggests that:

> the typical police personality is thought to include authoritarianism, suspicion, racism, hostility, insecurity, conservatism, and cynicism. (p.500)

This would make for interesting recruitment posters, but Brown and Willis (1985) were able to demonstrate that police recruits were less authoritarian after training, and had similar levels of authoritarianism to a control group of fire service recruits. Most police recruits are attracted to the profession because of the interest and variety inherent in the job together with the financial benefits rather than less savoury motives, but it may be that a combination of a powerful police culture and years of experience in a very demanding job take their toll. Without comprehensive longitudinal research on the psychological effects of a police career it is not yet possible to draw viable conclusions about a police personality.

Police officers need a range of competencies to perform the many different duties required of them, but identifying the core attributes required can be problematic, as can be the weighting of these attributes. The potential of police training programmes also needs to be taken into account since a poor score on a particular measure could be easily addressed by specific training, rather than overall rejection. Additionally, because the police select their managers from within the organisation, the recruitment process needs to be able to identify candidates who show leadership potential, while also recruiting the varied lower ranks. A key problem is that a detailed job analysis of the role of police officer is rarely carried out – assumptions are made but not tested, and insufficient consideration is given to the developing role of the police force which is necessary to reflect societal changes.

The procedures involved in promotion and selection for specialist roles can be equally problematic. For instance, officers who are authorised to carry firearms have to complete a psychological assessment process designed to reject unsuitable candidates, and if this process is ineffective the consequences could be fatal (Mirrlees-Black, 1992). Increasing recognition of the need to use high quality selection procedures at all levels, not least in relation to equal opportunities, has led many police forces to employ occupational psychologists as consultants and to set up Assessment Centres, which can systematically evaluate individuals' strengths and weaknesses and their fitness for a particular role.

Interviewing suspects

Successful interviews with suspects which result in evidence that secures a prosecution are probably the most effective way individual police officers can secure prominence in an investigation. Interviewing suspects has therefore acquired almost mythical status in terms of individuals' persuasive powers. Unfortunately in the past some of these methods of persuasion have resulted in innocent people confessing to crimes they did not commit, possibly as a result of police officers assuming that if a suspect is being interviewed they must be guilty otherwise they would not have been arrested (Moston et al, 1992). A prime example is the case of Peter Fell who was released in December 2000 after serving 17 years imprisonment for the murder of two Hampshire women in 1982. Mr Fell was denied access to a solicitor or a doctor despite his repeated requests and was held incommunicado by detectives for 54 hours, during which time he made a confession which was subsequently deemed unsafe. Psychiatric evidence showed that he was highly suggestible, and the appeal judges reviewing his case said:

> They (the police) allowed their quest for a conviction to override their responsibilities to an accused, and particularly to a vulnerable accused. If that fundamental right (of access to a solicitor) had not been denied, a false confession would not have been made.

Securing a confession has been seen as the major objective of interviewing suspects, rather than obtaining valuable information and eliminating the innocent and the vulnerable. The methods the suspect uses to dissuade police assumptions of guilt may be interpreted as further evidence of guilt, not unlike the interpretations made by nurses of the pseudopatients in Rosenhan's famous study *On being sane in insane places* (1973).

Theme link to Perspectives and Issues

(usefulness of psychological research)

Rosenhan (1973) asked his sane participants to try to gain admission to psychiatric hospitals. They all complained of hearing voices and of feeling 'empty', but otherwise the details they provided about themselves were accurate. Following admission these 'pseudopatients' stopped displaying symptoms and participated in ward activities, spending a lot of time writing notes about their experiences.

The most common diagnosis was schizophrenia and Rosenhan's participants remained in hospital for 7–52 days, unable to convince anyone that they were not mentally ill. Their note-taking behaviour and nervousness were seen to be symptomatic of their condition.

Rosenhan concluded that the staff were operating according to expectations developed from inflexible labels of sanity and insanity, to the extent that once a medical label had been attached all subsequent behaviour was interpreted according to that label. His research showed that mistaken diagnoses could have terrible consequences and that the assessment skills of admissions staff needed attention.

• **Figure 5.2:** Young offender being interviewed with his probation officer present

Police officers have often believed they have superior powers in detecting deception in suspects (Oxford, 1991), despite research which suggests that they are no better than civilians at being able to spot when someone is lying (Vrij, 1998). There is evidence to suggest that police officers place undue reliance on the general appearance of suspects to assist them in detecting deception, and while this may be the result of a tendency to stereotype, these cues are not reliable indicators of culpability.

The Police and Criminal Evidence Act (PACE) 1984 brought about significant changes in procedure, requiring all suspect interviews to be tape recorded. While this ensured that inappropriate interview methods could no longer be used, the success rate of interviews did not increase. Baldwin (1993) found that only 3% of suspects who originally denied charges eventually confessed, and that suspects changed their stories in only 10% of cases. This is in marked contrast to the way interviews are portrayed in police dramas, when suspects are depicted as suspicious, aggressive and largely unco-operative. In fact research indicates that most suspects give full answers to questions and are in the main polite and compliant (Pearse and Gudjonsson, 1996).

The introduction of PACE reduced the use of coercive methods of interrogation but there were other additional benefits. Fewer interviews were conducted at night, suspects were allowed easier access to solicitors, and there were fewer repeat interviews (Williamson, 1990, cited in Ainsworth, 2000). Jurors could listen to the tapes and make up their own minds as to whether suspects had been interviewed appropriately.

In spite of improved interview methods, some people may make false confessions not as a result of police pressure but because of some psychological deficit. Police officers therefore need to be able to distinguish these individuals from genuine suspects. Those who make false confessions may be suffering from mental illness, or they may feel guilty about something else entirely and want to obtain relief from admission.

Gudjonsson (1992) suggests there are two other types of suspect who may enter a false confession. The first he describes as **coerced-compliant**, those individuals who confess in order to end what has become an intolerable experience, the interview itself. Those people who feel intense pressure in certain situations will be unable to control their stress levels and admit guilt as an escape. Although they will probably retract this admission once they are out of the interview situation it may become very difficult to subsequently convince others of their innocence. A prime example of this is Stephen Downing who was released on appeal in 2001 after serving 27 years in prison for the murder of a young woman which he claimed throughout his trial and sentence that he did not commit. Downing was unable to apply for parole during ten years of eligibility because his continued protestations of innocence were interpreted as evidence that he was in denial.

Coerced-internalised is the second type identified by Gudjonsson (1992) and refers to vulnerable individuals who initially claim their innocence but during the course of interviewing come to accept the police version of events and confess. This may be because they have no reliable recall of events and are therefore suggestible, particularly if apparently irrefutable evidence is presented. Those people who are highly suggestible tend to share similar characteristics of trusting authority figures and low confidence levels (Ofshe, 1989). Gudjonsson (1989) claims that the four members of the Birmingham Six who falsely confessed to planting pub bombs had higher scores on his suggestibility scale than the two who did not confess.

Interviewing witnesses

A vital part of effective law enforcement is the ability of police officers to obtain detailed and accurate information from witnesses. Police interviewers need to enhance witnesses' recall without compromising reliability, and psychologists have been able to offer research-supported advice on maximising the effectiveness of investigative interviewing (Milne and Bull, 1999). Perhaps the best example of effective co-operation between psychologists and the police has been the incorporation of the **Cognitive Interview Technique** (CIT), developed by Fisher and Geiselman (1992), prompting Memon (1998) to say:

> The cognitive interview emerges as probably the most exciting development in the field of eyewitness testimony in the last 10 years. (p.183)

Traditionally police officers questioned potential witnesses and victims using a standard procedure which involved a period of free recall about the event followed by specific questions arising from the free recall stage. The balance of power was very evident, with the police officer in charge of the situation. No finesse was applied in terms of using systematic interview techniques which might improve both the amount of information recalled and the accuracy of that information. The CIT was developed to do precisely this and involves a shifting of the power balance whereby the interviewer facilitates the process of guided retrieval which is specifically designed to access information.

Theme link to Perspectives and Issues (**cognitive psychology**)

Fisher and Geiselman (1992) suggest the use of four main cognitive techniques which can produce a 50% improvement in information retrieval with no loss of accuracy in comparison to standard police interviews:

• *reinstating the context*
It is well established that memory is context-dependent (Godden & Baddeley, 1975), and so asking a witness to think about how they were feeling just before and during the event to be recalled, perhaps evoking the sounds and smells relating to the event, should facilitate retrieval.
• *focused concentration*
Persuading the witness to concentrate very hard on the task and focus on all the sensory details, even those considered trivial or irrelevant, should improve recall.
• *multiple retrieval attempts*
Encouraging a witness who feels they have recalled everything about an event to have another attempt can unlock previously unrecovered detail simply because of a confident assertion that there is more to be retrieved.
• *varied retrieval*
Witnesses will often recall events in chronological order, but if they are asked to recall details in a different order, or from a different perspective, this may trigger additional information.

The CIT has proved successful with a range of witnesses, including children, which explains why its principles have been adopted widely (Memon, 1998). However, the technique is time consuming and police officers need specific training from professional psychologists.

False allegations of crime

What if there is a suspicion that someone is making up their report of a crime and the police need to establish the validity of the allegation? A technique called **statement analysis** was developed by German psychologists to test the truthfulness of witness statements, particularly in cases of child sexual abuse (Gudjonsson, 1992). The basis of this technique is an assumption of quantifiable differences between genuine and fictitious accounts. Identifying these key features, which include originality, clarity, vividness, internal consistency, specific detail, subjective feelings, and spontaneous correction, is said to enable trained police officers to assess the validity of allegations. The technique has subsequently been refined (Steller and Koehnken, 1989), and research suggests that it can be a very useful strategy for assessing the credibility of witness statements (Marxsen, Yuille and Nisbett 1995).

Few (2001) proposes that the technique could be used to assess the truthfulness of rape allegations, suggesting that the differences between genuine and fictitious accounts of rape include the amount of detail given by alleged victims, and their willingness to blame themselves for the crime. Genuine victims will see nothing wrong in admitting they cannot remember every detail, and will talk about their emotions at the time, and the attacker's possible motive. They will also tend to include superfluous detail, and place the rape in the context of their own lives. In contrast, those who are making false claims will provide a bare account, confining themselves to a description of the event and will not blame themselves. Few developed a list of these differences, trained 16 police officers in using the technique, and then gave them eight rape allegation statements to assess, four of which were genuine and four fabricated. The 16 trained officers made a correct assessment in 72% of cases, while 16 untrained officers managed only a 50% success rate.

While this type of research can undoubtedly benefit police investigation, the low reporting, prosecution and conviction rate for both child abuse and rape suggests that statement analysis might better be used to assess the credibility of statements made by accused individuals rather than possible victims.

Tackling crime

Rising reported crime levels and decreasing clear-up rates have forced the police to set clear and accountable targets for their activities and to prioritise their efforts. Increasingly sophisticated methods of data collection and analysis have allowed the development of particular techniques, such as crime pattern analysis, which can be very effective in establishing links between crimes and in predicting future offences. This then allows the police to target particular areas at specific times. An interesting example of this is provided by Forrester, Frenz, O'Connor and Pease (1990) who identified a pattern of crime whereby certain properties on a Manchester housing estate were burgled twice over a short period. A cocoon Neighbourhood Watch scheme was then set up involving properties nearest the target homes. At the same time the council made these properties more secure, and the police patrolled specific areas rather than patrolling the estate generally. Burglaries on this particular estate were reduced by an impressive 75%, and the concept of repeat victimization gained a currency which attracted considerable research funding.

A variety of police strategies for reducing crime have now been evaluated, and Jordan (1998) suggests that the following interventions are effective:

- targeting repeat offenders in high-risk places, thereby securing convictions and long prison sentences.
- targeting repeat victims, as outlined by Forrester *et al*. (1990), and Pease (1998).
- directing police presence to known 'hot-spots', though saturation patrols can produce unease in some communities.

General approaches which seem to have considerable potential are improving police legitimacy within the community by reducing fear and suspicion of the police and treating the public with respect. **Problem-oriented policing** (POP), which involves the police resolving problems in the community rather than simply responding to calls, is also seen as an effective way forward (Read and Tilley, 2000).

Coping with the demands of the job

Police officers have a difficult job, and stress counselling together with strategies for avoiding burnout have become part of ongoing police training. White and Honig (1995) emphasise the need for a preventive approach which they call **wellness training**, assisting officers to consider lifestyle changes which will enable them to manage the stressors which accompany the job. Wellness training occurs against a backdrop of police culture which has traditionally denied the effects of stress, emphasising instead toughness, invulnerability, and the suppression of emotion. Specific topics included in wellness training are: managing people with mental illness; increasing cross-cultural awareness; improving communication skills; resisting dependency on alcohol; prioritising personal relationships; and psychologically surviving critical incidents, such as a fellow officer being injured.

Summary

It is clear that despite the often fragile relationship between psychologists and the police there is considerable benefit developing a closer relationship. Maintaining an effective 'thin blue line defending against chaos', as Reiner (1997) described the function of the police, can be a demanding and stressful occupation, but one which can profit from interdependent research designed to improve efficiency and reduce crime.

KEY TERMS

**police canteen culture
the police personality
psychometric testing
the person-situation debate
coerced-compliant suspects
coerced-internalised suspects
the cognitive interview
statement analysis
problem-oriented policing (POP)
wellness training**

EXERCISE **1**

Think of all the different aspects of a police officer's role, e.g.

Dog handler
Bomb disposal expert
Chief Constable
Drug Squad member
Undercover work
Domestic Violence Unit member
Child Protection Unit member
Road accident investigator
Riot Squad member
Reception duty
Vice Squad member
Court duty
Community work
Interviewer
Administrator

What different abilities and skills are important for each of these
roles, and how might each one be assessed by psychologists?

EXERCISE **2**

When Ainsworth (1995) asked police officers to list the qualities of a good recruit in order of importance they said:

a sense of humour, communication skills, adaptability, common sense, resilience, assertiveness, sensitivity, tolerance, integrity, literacy, honesty, and problem-solving ability.

Do you agree with this order, and how might these qualities reliably be measured?

EXERCISE **3**

Think of a few dramas you have watched which feature police officer characters, e.g. *The Vice, Cracker, Morse, A Touch of Frost, Silent Witness, Touching Evil, Second Sight, In Deep*. What characteristics did these officers display? Was the development of particular attitudes seen to be specific to individuals or the job itself? How was individual vulnerability dealt with?

EXERCISE **4**

How might you most effectively advertise for police officers who will represent the communities they serve?

six The psychology of testimony

One of the most important areas in which psychology has been applied to the courtroom is **eyewitness testimony**. It should not therefore be surprising that more empirical studies have been reported in this area of forensic psychology than in any other area.

> Nowhere are the problems of generalisability and reliability of research findings more acute than in the study of eyewitnessing. (Davies, 1992, p.265)

IN THIS CHAPTER WE WILL EXAMINE:

- cognitive processes and testimony
- variables influencing accurate identification of suspects
- aids to recall and recognition
- photofits and identity parades.

The accuracy of memory is important in many situations, but it is absolutely critical in one, namely a courtroom. Here the very life of the defendant may depend on the accuracy of a witness's or a victim's recall of events, and a jury's willingness to believe them. Eyewitness testimony and eyewitness identification play profoundly important roles in the apprehension and prosecution of criminal offenders. Jurors and police officers attach considerable importance to the evidence of eyewitnesses, despite generally accepted knowledge that there have been many cases of mistaken identification. Why should this be so? Juries and the police want hard evidence and they also want to believe the words of someone who was there at the time of the offence. Who else knows better than an eyewitness whose evidence is compelling? Unfortunately, as Cutler and Penrod (1995) point out, eyewitnesses can be '100% confident and still be 100% wrong'.

An example of this was the case of Ed Honaker. Wells *et al.* (1998) describe another 40 cases where DNA evidence subsequently showed that none of the convicted criminals could have been the true offender. It is generally believed therefore that eyewitness identification is the leading cause of false convictions. A word of advice? Don't volunteer to stand in an identity parade or line-up. In 20% of the line-ups studied by Wright and McDaid (1996) the witness identified an innocent foil whom the police had chosen to stand with the suspect.

The case of Ed Honaker and misidentification Ed Honaker was released in 1994 after serving 10 years in a Virginia prison for rape. He was convicted on the basis of eyewitness testimony from the victim together with her identification of him from mugshots. Honaker protested his innocence over several years, and the Innocence Project (a group of lawyers and law students who re-examine convicted cases) eventually took up his case and lodged an appeal. They revealed that the victim had had hypnosis to enhance her memory of the rape (which is illegal), and that Honaker's photograph in the mugshots had differed from all the others because of the background, thus increasing the probability of its selection. Additionally they presented DNA analysis which revealed that Honaker could not have been the rapist.

Loftus (1974) very clearly demonstrated the mistaken faith jurors can put in eyewitness testimony. She gave participants three versions of a robbery and murder case, and asked them to decide whether the defendant was guilty. Circumstantial evidence which was presented to the mock jurors included the fact that

- the robber ran into the defendant's apartment block
- money was found in the defendant's room
- tests revealed there was a slight chance the defendant had fired a gun on the day of the robbery-murder.

Only 18% of participants hearing just this information said the defendant was guilty. Another group of participants was given the circumstantial evidence plus another piece of evidence – the store clerk's eyewitness identification of the defendant. Of these, 72% were prepared to convict the defendant, demonstrating the powerful effect of eyewitness testimony. Nothing that surprising? Rather more striking were the results of a third condition in Loftus's study in which participants received the circumstantial evidence plus the eyewitness testimony plus information discrediting the witness – that he was short-sighted, he was not wearing his glasses at the time of the offence, and he could not have seen the robber's face from where he was standing. Nevertheless, 68% of the mock jurors still convicted.

The weight attached to eyewitness testimony may be because intuitively we think of memory and perception as passive copying processes, rather like a camera or tape recorder which provides a permanent record of events and simply needs to be replayed. Contemporary psychological research in fact shows both memory and perception to be active and constructive processes. Perception does not produce a record, but an interpretation dependent on prior beliefs and attitudes, while memory is susceptible to both deterioration and reconstruction.

How reliable is human memory?

During the nineteenth century the fallibility of human memory in identification cases was recognised by William James who said, 'testimony to personal identity is proverbially fallacious' (1890, p.97) and as prominent researchers in the area of eyewitness testimony have said: 'Human memory is a fragile and elusive creature. It can be supplemented, partially restructured, or even completely altered by post-event inputs.' (Loftus and Ketcham, p.168)

Post-event information can affect recall quite significantly, as Loftus & Palmer (1974) vividly demonstrated. In one study participants watched a film of a car accident and filled in a questionnaire afterwards. Some of them were asked,

The influence of post-event information on recall

'About how fast were the cars going when they *hit* each other?'

while others were asked,

'About how fast were the cars going when they *smashed* into each other?'

The second group made significantly higher estimates of the speed of the cars. One week later all participants were brought back and asked,

'Did you see any broken glass?'

There was in fact no broken glass, but those who had received the previous question with 'smashed' in it were more likely to say they had indeed seen some glass (32% versus 14%).

Even very subtle changes in wording can have an effect. Loftus and Zanni (1975) showed subjects a short film of a road accident. Some of them were asked,

'Did you see *a* broken headlight?'

while others were asked,

'Did you see *the* broken headlight?'

There was actually no broken headlight in the film, but 7% of those asked about *a* broken headlight said they had seen it, and 17% asked about *the* broken headlight said they had seen it.

The work on post-event influences supports the assertions made by Bartlett (1932) in relation to the 'effort after meaning' which we tend to employ when remembering past events. Bartlett suggested that we try to make past events meaningful in order to make sense of ambiguity or uncertainty. Loftus (1979), however, found that if the misleading information introduced to participants was 'blatantly incorrect' it had little effect on recall, and no attempt at imposing meaning was made.

There are other factors which can interfere with recall and make witnesses suggestible. One is **source monitoring error** where imagination and reality get confused (Johnson, Hashtroudi and Lindsay, 1993). For instance, when Crombag *et al.* (1996) asked people if they remembered seeing the film clip of a Boeing 747 crashing into an Amsterdam block of apartments, 60% said yes even though no film had been taken of the crash. They had presumably heard so many news reports of the incident that they had formed an image of what might have happened, making them suggestible to the idea that they might have watched video footage of the event.

How does emotion affect memory?

Most crimes involve intense emotions of fear and anger so witnesses' recall of such incidents are inevitably affected by such feelings. However, there is disagreement about the effect of emotion on memory. On the one hand there is the belief that experiencing a highly emotional event produces what Brown and Kulik (1977) describe as **flashbulb memories** or an exact trace, such as where we were when we heard news of a famous person's death. On the other hand is the belief that highly emotional events are repressed because they can be damaging. It is this belief which lies at the heart of the recovered memory debate – that memories of child abuse can be released through therapy many years after the event.

• **Figure 6.1:** Flashbulb memory: Where were you when you heard of Diana's death?

Neither of these two extremes seems to be entirely correct. Heightened emotion does not appear to make people forget. Traumatic amnesia is rare and can usually be explained by head injury or youth (Pope, Oliva and Hudson, 1999). Indeed, experiencing stress tends to improve memory for central details, though often at the expense of peripheral details which may subsequently be embellished (Christianson, 1992). In the literature of eyewitness testimony this funnelling of attention is called **weapon focus**, because when an offender holds a gun or a knife this tends to concentrate witnesses' attention and improves subsequent memory at the expense of other details, such as the suspect's face (Loftus, Loftus and Messo, 1987).

The view that memory for emotive events is fairly good is supported by real world research. For example Yuille and Cutshall (1986) describe interviews conducted with 13 witnesses of a violent street crime 4–5 months after they had been interviewed by the police. The results of both interviews were then compared and revealed considerable accuracy, despite the introduction of two misleading questions. Significantly, those witnesses who appeared to be the most distressed by their experience (for example, those who reported suffering nightmares) were the most accurate in their recall.

Recognising and identifying faces

The recognition and identification of faces is a very specific area of research in eyewitness testimony. Goldstein and Chance (1971) tested subjects for their recall of photos of women's faces, snowflakes, and inkblots. Participants were shown 14 photos from each set, and tested immediately afterwards, and then again after 48 hours. The results showed that accuracy of recall for faces was good – 71%, as against 48% for inkblots, and 33% for snowflakes. Facial recall and recognition are, however, quite complex aspects of memory. For instance, most of us can easily recognise a familiar face, but if we were asked to describe that face in detail would experience some difficulty. Moreover, while we may often recognise a face as familiar we may not be able to pinpoint why, or recall the person's name.

In real life these problems associated with facial recall can have serious consequences. A vivid example concerns an Australian psychologist, Donald Thompson, whose research attracted some media attention, and he appeared in several TV programmes to discuss his findings. A few weeks later, however, he was picked up by the police, put in a line-up, and identified by a woman who claimed he had raped her. It subsequently emerged that the time of the rape had coincided with Thompson's participation in a live TV discussion, providing him with an excellent alibi. The woman had been attacked while this programme was on air, and although she correctly identified Thompson's face, having emotionally associated it with the event, she wrongly assigned it to the rapist. This can be regarded as unconscious transference of memory traces.

Media coverage of crime can play a part in this type of unconscious transference. For instance, Ainsworth (1995) showed participants a local news story about a series of sexual assaults which included two photos, one a photofit of the suspect and the other a photograph of a 'good samaritan' who had helped one of the victims. A week later the participants were asked to select the suspect from a selection of six photos. One group was shown a selection containing the photofit of the suspect, a second group was shown a selection containing the photo of the 'good samaritan', while the third group was shown a random selection. The first group picked the suspect on almost 40% of occasions, while the second group incorrectly selected the face of the 'good samaritan' on 50% of of occasions. The chances of selecting the suspect or the 'good samaritan' were roughly equal, suggesting that unconscious transference was playing a part.

Labelling a face can also influence how people recall facial features. Shepherd, Davies and Ellis (1978) asked participants to view a photo of a male face for 30 seconds and then asked them to construct a photofit. Half of them were told the face belonged to the brave captain of a lifeboat, while the other half were told the face was that of a mass murderer. The subsequent

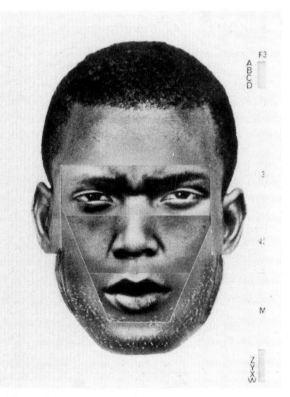

• **Figure 6.2:** An example of a photofit

photofit pictures were quite different, with the face of the alleged mass murderer judged to be more cruel, unpleasant and unintelligent.

Photofits were first introduced in the UK in 1970 and involve trained operators selecting alternatives for specific facial features to match a witness's verbal description until they have produced a type likeness. Subsequent refinements have included *Mac-A-Mug* and *EvoFIT*, which incorporate the benefits of computer software and graphics in generating images while recognising that people are good at recognising faces but not good at accurately describing features. With *EvoFIT* witnesses look at computer-generated images, starting with random face shapes and features, and are asked to select the ones most closely resembling the subject. Each time the witness makes a selection, a new set of increasingly detailed photographs is created, combining the characteristics of those chosen. While these methods are widely used there has been little in the way of their evaluation, nor has there been much recognition of the possibility that producing such a likeness may interfere with a witness's original memory.

When witnesses experience problems recalling faces they may be presented with a 'mugshot file' which is a collection of photos of people

Theme link to Perspectives and Issues (**developmental psychology**) and Methodology

In studies with young children there is often a power dimension which can affect the findings, and in some ways it is not surprising that children being interviewed by adults might be suggestible. Children tend to want to please adults, who they believe know everything already. For instance, if a child is being interviewed by an adult and is asked to pick out a photograph of someone they have met, they are likely to assume that if the grown-up has gone to the trouble of setting out a display of photographs, the correct one will probably be there. Peters (1987) found exactly that. He asked children who had visited the dentist (a situation of mild stress) to pick out from a range of photographs someone they had seen there. In one condition the target photograph was present, but the children selected a different photograph 31% of the time. However, when the target photograph was not included in the selection, the children picked one of the photographs 71% of the time. Very few of them were prepared to say they were not sure and then pick none.

Studies carried out with children in particular developmental stages therefore need to take account of this possible effect in the methodology.

already known to the police, on the assumption that these photos may act as a prompt. One of the problems associated with mugshot files, however, is that the witness may feel under pressure to make a selection even though they do not feel particularly confident. This was certainly the case with the child participants in a study by Peters (1987). Another problem is that the witness is being asked to view a static representation of a suspect whom they saw live.

The same problems can occur when a witness is presented with a photospread or a show-up. A **show-up** is the presentation of a photo of one suspect for the witness to identify, and is the least satisfactory form of identification, though as Ainsworth (2000) points out, one form of show-up is used consistently in courtrooms without question. This occurs when witnesses are asked to point out the perpetrator in court, but it presumes automatically that the right person is in the dock, since the witness is highly unlikely to choose someone in the public gallery. With show-ups witnesses may be led to believe that the police are very confident about the suspect since this is the only one being presented. Yarmey (1992), however, was able to show that only 57% of witnesses in a show-up were able to correctly identify a person with whom they had interacted two minutes earlier. A photospread is more effective than a show-up, as it involves the presentation of at least 12 faces all resembling the suspect. Much, however, will depend on the fair selection of foils alongside the suspect, and the witness may still experience pressure to make a selection, possibly being unprepared to admit that the suspect is not present.

HOW RELIABLE ARE LINE-UPS OR IDENTITY PARADES?

Witnesses who have picked out a suspect from a mugshot file or a photospread may then be asked to select a suspect from an **identity parade** or **line-up**, where the suspect is presented live alongside a number of foils. The problem here is that witnesses may want to appear consistent and therefore automatically select the same person they identified from the mug-shots. This may mean they are doubly wrong, but their actions might be interpreted as confirming evidence. Witnesses are often traumatised victims too and may therefore be motivated to make a live choice which is closest to their memory, or just the most likely from the selection offered.

Suspects are allowed to choose their own position in the line-up, but they may still present quite differently to the foils. They may appear nervous and stressed and if their anxiety is communicated via non-verbal indicators, witnesses may base their selection on this information. The similarity of the foils to the suspect is crucial, but there is little evidence of how this is regulated, and during particularly emotive investigations the pressure will be on to secure an identification as quickly as possible. If the suspect has an unusual appearance it will be even more difficult to find physically similar foils. Legal challenges are often made on the grounds that identification parades were not conducted fairly.

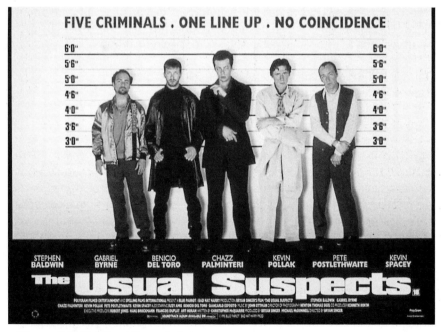

• **Figure 6.3:** The Usual Suspects line-up

Witnesses often survey the line-up as a whole and then make their selection, but research suggests that a more accurate selection will be made if witnesses are presented with single faces in sequence and then asked whether each face belongs to the perpetrator or not (Thomson, 1995).

CROSS-RACE IDENTIFICATION

We have already noted that perception can be influenced by prior beliefs and attitudes. Even support for different football clubs seems to affect perception, as Hastorf and Cantril (1954) demonstrated. They showed a film of a football game to fans from both sides and asked them to count instances of inappropriate behaviour and fouls. Guess the result? Each group of fans reported many more fouls from the opposing side.

Racial prejudice can very easily affect the way the world is viewed, as was vividly demonstrated by Duncan (1976) (see below). Chance and Goldstein (1996) have shown that identifying faces from a different ethnic group is more difficult than identifying faces from one's own group, because of inappropriate and unfamiliar encoding strategies. The area of cross-race identification thus produces a particularly problematic issue in evaluating eyewitness testimony.

Theme link to Perspectives and Issues (**social psychology**)

Duncan (1976) was interested in the effect of stereotypes on perception. White participants were asked to view a video of a disagreement between two people which resulted in one pushing the other. In fact four versions of the video were shown to different groups:

Tape 1 (White assailant/white victim)
Tape 2 (White assailant/black victim)
Tape 3 (Black assailant/white victim)
Tape 4 (Black assailant/black victim)

Participants were asked whether the behaviour of the person who pushed the other could best be described as 'playing around' or as 'violent behaviour'. When the perpetrator was black, 70% of participants described his behaviour as violent, while only 13% of participants chose this descriptor when the perpetrator was white. The attribution of violence was highest for Tape 3, and lowest for Tape 1.

AIDS TO RECALL

One of the best examples of psychological knowledge and police expertise coming together has been the development of the **cognitive interview** as a means of improving witness recall (see Chapter Five on The Police and Crime).

The technique was first developed by Geiselman *et al*. (1984) as a response to requests from police officers for assistance in improving witness interviews. Based on well-established psychological principles of the guided retrieval of information from memory by the use of specific techniques, it was modified to take into account the social and practical aspects of managing an interview situation. In training officers to use the cognitive interview, it was recognised that implementing the retrieval strategies effectively also required the development of specific social and communication skills. These included facilitating the 'transfer of control' from the interviewer to the witness by establishing rapport, the use of open-ended questions which require a detailed response, positive encouragement and no interruptions (Memon and Stevenage, 1996).

Most studies which evaluate the use of the cognitive interview confirm that it can produce more information than a traditional interviewing style without any loss of accuracy (Fisher and Geiselman, 1992), and is most effective when used by trained officers with motivated and co-operative adult witnesses. The complexity of the technique can make it unsuitable for very young children, though Loohs (1996) reports a positive outcome using the cognitive interview together with toy props with a group of six-year-old children.

Summary

Research seems to demonstrate that eyewitness testimony, while sometimes compelling, is not always as reliable as the police and jurors believe. Witnesses are susceptible to influences at various stages during their observation and recall of an event, and are also vulnerable to incorrect post-event information. In view of this it seems clear that eyewitness testimony should never be allowed as the sole evidence supporting a conviction, although psychologists can greatly assist the police in developing interview techniques which can improve the extent and the accuracy of witnesses' recall. Perhaps psychologists should also be allowed to appear as expert witnesses, in order to advise jurors of the dangers of too readily accepting the testimony of eyewitnesses.

KEY TERMS

eyewitness testimony
post-event information
source monitoring error
flashbulb memory
weapon focus
identity parade
line-up
photospread/mugshot file
show-up
cognitive interview

EXERCISE 1

Why do you think juries put so much faith in the evidence of eyewitnesses to crime?

EXERCISE 2

Since it would be ethically unacceptable to subject child, or indeed adult, participants to distress, how might psychologists create a situation whereby they can measure children's responses to questions after a stressful experience without breaching ethical procedures?

EXERCISE 3

If you were a psychologist and you were asked to advise jurors how they should evaluate eyewitness testimony, what studies would you describe to them?

seven

The psychology of the courtroom

The courtroom is the dramatic centrepiece of the criminal justice system where the actors include the accused, the victim, lawyers, witnesses, legal clerks, magistrates, judges, jurors, and the public gallery. All these actors will follow a script which relies on their past experience, and the role to which they have been allocated. The social psychology of the courtroom as drama has proved a rich source of data for investigators. This chapter will focus on:

- trial procedures and persuasion techniques
- jury selection and decision-making
- children as witnesses.

The decisions which are made in the courtroom can have devastating effects on many people, and yet by and large the processes by which these decisions are reached have not always been fully understood. Psychologists have systematically examined these processes in an attempt to determine contributory factors, and some of their findings have cast doubt on, among other things, the reliability of the jury system, and the testimony of child witnesses. Their methods of investigation, however, have often had to fall short of ecological validity because of legal constraints in observing and interviewing real jurors, and ethical constraints in interviewing child witnesses about alleged sexual abuse.

Juries

Trial by jury – the concept of impartial judgement of alleged offenders by their peers or equals – has long been enshrined as a noble component of English law.

No freeman shall be seized, or imprisoned, or disposed or outlawed, or in any way destroyed; nor will we condemn him, nor will we commit him to prison, excepting by the lawful judgement of his peers, or by the law of the land. (Clause 39, Magna Carta, 1215)

Recent events, when the decisions of juries have been overturned by Appeal Judges, together with government moves to restrict trial by jury for certain offences only, have caused considerable concern. However, studies of actual jury verdicts and the outcomes of psycholegal research into jury decision-making suggest that the jury system is not always a reliable method for determining guilt or innocence.

Legislation has made it quite difficult for psychologists to study the way in which real juries make decisions, and so a variety of methods have been developed. These include '**shadow juries**' and '**mock juries**' which simulate what goes on in the jury room, but also allow variables to be manipulated so that particular hypotheses can be tested, for instance the influence of the defendant's race or gender. A 'shadow jury' might sit in the public gallery during a trial and then discuss the case as if they were a real jury, while a 'mock jury' would be asked to watch a video of a court case and then reach a verdict. In both cases the decision-making of the group is carefully monitored and then analysed. These methods have been criticised because they can in no way replicate the experience of an actual jury – participants are often volunteer undergraduates, and their decisions have no real impact (Hans, 1992). Nonetheless, the findings of these studies cannot be ignored. Essentially juries are small groups and as such are subject to the same psychological processes that all groups experience when they have to interact and reach decisions.

WHO SITS ON JURIES?

While no qualifications are required to sit on a jury (other than age and the right to vote) and one might therefore assume that the first twelve people selected would form the jury, there are procedures by which objections may be made to a limited number of potential individual jurors. Objections can be made by both prosecution and defence and are often based on assumptions about the personalities, attitudes and beliefs of potential jurors which it is believed may influence their judgement. American lawyers routinely call upon the services of psychologists during what is called a *voir dire* hearing to select jurors who they believe will be sympathetic to their client, though Kadane (1993) suggests that there is often agreement between defence and prosecution as to which potential jurors should be rejected. In 1995 a popular black former athlete and entertainer, O.J. Simpson, was tried for the murder of his white wife. Both prosecution and defence lawyers were very concerned about the pre-trial media coverage and so they asked potential jurors to complete a 75 page questionnaire indicating their prior knowledge of the case and their attitudes to various issues before considering their eligibility. As

• **Figure 7.1:** O.J. Simpson, left, in a Los Angeles courtroom with his attorney just after the prosecution rested its case in his double-murder trial (1995)

things turned out (O.J. Simpson was surprisingly acquitted), Marcia Clark, the prosecution lawyer, seriously underestimated the sympathies of American black female jurors. It is also apparent that jurors who desperately want to be selected can simply conceal the truth during *voir dire* (Seltzer *et al.*, 1991).

Factors which could influence juror selection by defence lawyers might include the importance of choosing jurors with similar backgrounds to the client (on the assumption that we like people who are similar to us), and body language and physical appearance which might indicate 'strength' or 'weakness', since a weak juror may be more easily influenced (Mauet and McCrimmon, 1993). Gender can play a role, with female jurors more likely to convict a defendant charged with rape (Bagby, Parker, Rector and Kalemba, 1994). Younger jurors are more likely to acquit, whereas highly educated jurors are more likely to convict (Hans and Vidmar, 1982).

The choice of a foreperson is the first task a jury has to undertake, and this individual can exert considerable influence, especially when jurors have difficulty understanding the judge's instructions (Kagehiro, 1990). Hence, identifying a foreperson likely to be sympathetic to their case becomes crucial in jury selection. Most research suggests that middle-class males who initiate discussion tend to be elected as forepersons (Deosoran, 1993). Kerr *et al.* (1982) examined the records of 179 trials in San Diego and found that although 50% of jurors were female, 90% of forepersons were male. The first person who speaks is often chosen as foreperson, and when jurors debate around a rectangular table those who sit at the head of the table are more likely to be chosen than those seated in the middle (Strodtbeck *et al.*, 1957).

WHAT INFLUENCES JURORS?

Several studies indicate that jurors are influenced by a variety of non-legal characteristics of defendants, perhaps because of the way individual jurors construct a narrative to justify one verdict or another, and this involves them focusing on different kinds of information (Hastie, 1993). The attractiveness of the defendant appears to be one of these factors, with attractive defendants being dealt with less harshly (DeSantis and Kayson, 1997), unless they were perceived to have used their attractiveness in committing their offences (Sigall and Ostrove, 1975). Similarly, Downs and Lyons (1991) asked police escorts to rate the physical attractiveness of 1700 defendants appearing in Texas courts and found that judges imposed higher fines on the less attractive defendants.

Jurors are also more likely to be sympathetic towards defendants with whom they can identify. This might explain the findings of a national survey before the O.J. Simpson trial in which 77% of white respondents, but only 45% of black respondents, saw the case against him as 'fairly strong' (Smolowe, 1995). Racial bias does seem to be a factor in the range of influences on jurors, as Pfeifer and Ogloff (1991) demonstrated when their white participants judged black defendants guiltier than white defendants, especially when the victim was white. However, when participants were given specific instructions that each element of the offence had to be proven beyond reasonable doubt, the differences disappeared.

Gordon *et al.* (1988) showed that the effect of race can be complicated by the type of crime. They varied both the race of the defendant (black or white) and the type of crime supposedly committed (embezzlement or burglary). The white embezzler received a significantly longer sentence than the black embezzler but this situation was reversed for the burglary. It was suggested that this was because racial stereotypes for particular crimes were operating, with participants holding the black burglar and the white embezzler more responsible for their crimes.

The prior beliefs and attitudes of jurors can also influence their decisions (Krauss, 1995), and Ellsworth (1993) found that people who did not oppose the death penalty also tended to be biased towards the prosecution and more likely to return a guilty verdict. Any potential jurors in America who are opposed to the death penalty may be disqualified from jury service on the grounds that they would be unable to return a fair verdict, and it has been suggested that this is more likely to produce conviction-prone juries (Haney, 1993).

Although much research in the past has focused on juror characteristics, more contemporary research emphasises the interaction effect between juror characteristics and case characteristics, that is the quality of the evidence presented and the nature of the alleged offences.

HOW DO JURORS REACH THEIR VERDICTS?

There is an assumption that 'jury deliberation is a reliable way of establishing the truth in a contentious matter' (Stephenson, p.179), but it has been suggested that most jurors have already decided on a verdict before they retire to deliberate, and that the first ballot usually reveals a majority preference (Kalven and Zeisel, 1966). Pennington and Hastie (1990) disagree with this finding and suggest that the process towards achieving a final agreed verdict is much more complex, while Sandys and Dillehay (1995) surveyed 142 ex-jurors and revealed that an average of 45 minutes was spent discussing cases before a first ballot was taken.

In the jury room discussions it seems that those who talk the most are 'socially successful' jurors, men, and the foreperson (Ellsworth, 1993). The longer the jury is out the more likely it is they will acquit (Baldwin and McConville, 1980), and as discussion continues the minority are more likely to agree with the majority view.

Various mathematical models have been developed to explain the processes by which juries reach their decisions, but Pennington and Hastie (1993) suggest an alternative model in which jurors actively construct

• **Figure 7.2:** Henry Fonda in the film *Twelve Angry Men*. Even a minority of one can sway the opinion of a twelve person jury

explanations for the evidence presented to them in order to reach a verdict. This dynamic process is therefore entirely dependent on cognitive processes of selection, attention, interpretation and recall which relate to pre-existing schema, and this explains why two jurors presented with the same evidence can reach quite different verdicts. It also suggests that the influence of pre-trial publicity in terms of constructing possible narratives can be highly significant (see Freedman, Martin and Mota, 1998).

DO JURIES ALWAYS GET IT RIGHT?

Sometimes juries acquit a defendant even when they feel the case has been proven. This happens when jurors feel sympathy for the defendant, for instance in mercy killings, or when they feel a prosecution should not have been brought. For example in 2001, two anti-nuclear protesters were charged with conspiracy to cause criminal damage to a Trident submarine. Despite the judge telling the jury that ideals formed no defence against the charge the jurors brought in a verdict of not guilty.

In the most comprehensive review of jury decisions undertaken, Kalven and Zeisel (1966) suggested that in 78% of cases the jury's verdict was the same as that of the judge. However this still leaves a worrying number of cases where the wrong verdict might have been reached, with potentially devastating consequences. In cases where a majority verdict has been acceptable there may have been psychological factors, such as the pressure to **conform**, which might explain this outcome.

Theme link to Perspectives and Issues (**social psychology**)

The work of Solomon Asch (1956) on conformity suggests that in small groups there is often pressure exerted on dissenting individuals to conform, and while they may privately hold on to their original opinion, they may ultimately bow to the majority to avoid ridicule or rejection. This is the difference between informational influence, when people are genuinely persuaded by others who appear to be more knowledgeable, and normative influence when people go along with the group's majority view because they do not want to appear deviant.

Another social psychological process which can influence the way juries reach their decisions is **group polarisation** (originally posited as the risky shift phenomenon by Stoner, 1968) whereby whatever initial view is stated, this view becomes more exaggerated the longer the matter is discussed. Hastie *et al.* (1983) were able to demonstrate this by showing a re-enactment of a murder trial to 69 mock juries. Whatever the initial verdict preferences were for each jury, the length of the subsequent discussions strengthened these preferences.

Summary

Juries are groups, and are swayed by the same influences that bear upon other groups, rather than being objective arbiters of justice. Psychologists have only been able to study the group dynamics of juries by the use of methodologies, which have some weaknesses, but their findings have been of great benefit. Jurors are individuals who construct a story that explains the evidence by fitting the information presented into their existing schema, and who then participate in an intense discussion about their views. Their own characteristics may therefore be an influence on juror selection, but it is the dynamic between these characteristics and the case itself which will determine the outcome.

Children as witnesses

Whereas adult eyewitnesses tend to be believed, even in situations where a healthy scepticism might be more appropriate, the case has been very different for child witnesses. Prior to 1984 it was firmly believed that children make poorer witnesses than adults because their perception and memory are inferior, they cannot differentiate between fact and fantasy, and they are highly **suggestible** (Clifford, 1993). Subsequent research, however, has demonstrated that while there may be differences between the testimony offered by children and adults, the evidence supplied by children is not inevitably inferior and with appropriate interviewing techniques can become a significant component in successful prosecutions of sex offenders (see Westcott et al., 2001). The outcome of this psychological research has had a significant effect not only on the way children who have been victims of abuse are interviewed, but also on the way they are treated within the criminal justice system.

Until the introduction of legislation in the 1988, 1991 and 1996 Criminal Justice Acts, young children were simply not allowed to give evidence in court until they satisfied requirements that they understood their duty to tell the truth, and their evidence was corroborated. In addition judges were required to warn jurors of the dangers of believing children's evidence. Not surprisingly these factors ensured that many cases which relied on children's testimony collapsed. A notable example was in 1994 when two Newcastle nursery school assistants were charged with rape and indecent assault after several young children reported abuse. The judge halted the trial because he felt, after viewing the video interview with the eldest child (aged five), that the children were too young to give an intelligible account. He also had the 'gravest worry' as to whether he would allow his own young children to undergo cross-examination in similar circumstances. The two defendants were discharged, to the horror of the children's parents who had told their children they would be believed and protected if only they told the truth about what had happened to them.

RESEARCH FINDINGS

While it is true to say that children's recall improves with age, and that younger children provide less information than older children and adults (Clifford, 1993), contemporary research shows that previous beliefs that children's memory is inferior were unfounded. Fivush (1993) demonstrates that preschool children can provide accurate accounts over time of events they have experienced, though they tend to supply less detail than older children. However, with prompts and cues they can provide more information. The style of questioning is also important, as a child who is asked several different questions about the same event may feel they must be providing the wrong answer and become confused.

Bruck and Ceci (1995) have emphasised the power dimension in interviews between adults and children. Children may want to please the interviewer and thus provide an account which they believe the adult wants to hear. Equally they may be vulnerable to pressure to change their account and then provide fabrication which is repeated in later interviews.

IMPROVEMENTS IN LEGISLATION

The requirement for corroboration of a child's evidence has now been abolished, as has the need for a judge's warning to the jury, and children as young as three and four have been allowed to give evidence (Flin, 1993). There have also been welcome innovations, most notably the introduction of a live videolink in many courts. This allows children to give evidence from a room separate to the courtroom, and to be cross-examined via the live link, thus avoiding the stress which might be caused by facing the accused. Courts also now accept videotaped interviews with children as evidence, and these have the advantage of being recorded shortly after the charges are brought, so are more likely to be accurate and detailed. New legislation under the Youth Justice and Criminal Evidence Act will make it possible for cross-examination, as well as the initial interview, to be pre-recorded on video, though these measures will be subject to judicial discretion.

However, some problems still remain in relation to the difficulties faced by child victims. There is still a long waiting period before the trial – Davies and Noon (1991) estimate an average of ten months – and there have been concerns expressed about the reduced impact of evidence given by videolink. Ross et al.'s (1994) found that mock juries were more likely to convict if shown a child giving evidence in open court than if the same evidence was presented via videolink. The use of videotaped interviews has also been problematic as some early interviews were not conducted appropriately and contained leading questions which were then successfully challenged by the defence and ruled inadmissable.

Since videotaped interviews are not automatically accepted as evidence, a code of practice was developed after consultation with lawyers and psychologists, designed to advise those conducting interviews with children (**Memorandum of Good Practice**, Home Office, 1992). The main elements of this code are the need to:

Interviewing children appropriately

- assess the child's level of cognitive skills before drawing up a plan of the interview
- provide a welcoming and informal setting for the interview to alleviate stress and embarrassment
- position cameras and microphones so that the interviewer and the child can be seen at all times
- use an interviewer who has been appropriately trained to adopt an 'active listener' stance
- draw up an interview plan which establishes rapport between the interviewer and the child, explains the purpose of the interview to the child, and encourages the child to provide a free narrative account, with a minimum of open-ended prompting, e.g. 'and then what happened?'
- encourage more detail with the use of open-ended questions or specific but non-leading questions, e.g. 'was this in the morning or the afternoon?'
- close the interview positively.

Psychological expertise in effective interviewing techniques can be extremely useful in training police officers and social workers so that they can secure credible evidence (see Memon and Bull, 2000). Children often believe that because one adult (the accused) already knows what happened to them, all other adults must know too. It is therefore important for the interviewer to reassure the child that the real facts are not known, but if they are not able to remember all the facts they should say so. Where children have difficulties putting their thoughts into words, props such as anatomically correct dolls can be used, although Bruck and Ceci (1995) advise caution in the use of these props as children are often curious and may report having been touched when this is not the case. Dolls are probably only useful in enabling the child to mimic actions which they have already mentioned.

There are other advantages to the introduction of videotaped interviews, in that defendants can be shown parts of the tape during their police questioning. When they are faced with such evidence many defendants choose to change their plea to guilty. Liposvky et al. (1992) found that in only 17% of such cases did the child subsequently have to appear in court.

Summary

Most of the evidence suggests that children's ability to recall events and give evidence in court has been seriously underestimated in the past, and this has led to welcome innovations within the criminal justice system. A fundamental question remains, however, as to whether the welfare of damaged children and the interests of justice can ever be compatible. While psychological research might suggest more effective and therapeutic ways of dealing with child witnesses, there will always be a legal pull towards ensuring that defendants receive a fair hearing.

KEY TERMS

**mock juries
shadow juries
voir dire/juror selection
small group dynamics
conformity
group polarisation
suggestibility
Memorandum of Good Practice**

EXERCISE **1**

Divide yourselves into two groups and construct arguments for and against jury trials. Some examples might include:

For	Against
Twelve heads are better than one	The task is too important to leave to amateurs
Jurors use common sense	Juries cannot understand complex legal matters
Jury discussions result in a fair decision	Jurors can be nobbled

As a psychologist how might you investigate some of these assertions? What would be your hypotheses? Bear in mind the opposing views of juries as, on the one hand demonstrating democracy and freedom, while on the other undermining legal principles. These two views are demonstrated in the following quotes:

> What makes juries worthwhile is that they see things differently from the judges, that they can water the law, and the function which they filled two centuries ago as a corrective to the corruption and partiality of the judges requires essentially the same qualities as the function they perform today as an organ of the disestablishment. (Lord Devlin, 1978)

> The jury is an anti-democratic, irrational and haphazard legislator, whose erratic and secret decisions run counter to the rule of law. (Darbyshire, 1991)

EXERCISE 2

Answer this question, which has two parts:

a) Describe jury decision-making processes.
b) If you were a member of a jury, suggest what rules you might make for yourself to prevent you from reaching the wrong decision. Give reasons for your answer.

8 Offender punishments and treatments, and preventing crime

There has been considerable disagreement between academics, politicians and the public about what should be done with offenders, and how crime can be prevented. The contribution made by psychologists is in terms of developing intervention programmes which can reduce the chances of reoffending, and introducing strategies for developmental and environmental crime prevention. In this chapter we will focus on:

- the types and effectiveness of punishments
- offender treatment programmes
- crime prevention.

Punishment and treatment

While the public, and those politicians who respond only to public opinion, believe that those who commit offences should be punished, psychologists are committed to a belief that individuals can change and can be responsive to rehabilitative intervention within prison or in the community. Types of intervention which are likely to reduce reconviction rates include educating offenders, preparing them for employment, and increasing their personal effectiveness. What is most unlikely to do this is simply incarcerating offenders in prison and offering them neither training nor treatment. Lipsey (1992) found that imprisonment, boot camps and intense surveillance resulted in a 25% increase in reoffending rates on average, while Home Office statistics (1994) reveal a staggering reconviction rate of 82% for young adult males, who commit the majority of recorded crimes.

So, prison does not work, and yet in the past five years the UK prison population has risen from 44,000 to 66,000, with the Home Office predicting that it will hit an all-time high of 68,300 by March 2002. This despite a decrease in reported crime (Home Office, 2001). The picture for female offenders is no different, with the number of women being sent to prison having doubled in six years, rising to 3,392 in 1999.

Reducing prison numbers to the levels of the mid to late 1990s would save up to £500 million a year. It costs £25,000 per year to keep someone in prison, while community service costs £2,500. However, the courts are increasingly using prison as a deterrent despite the serious overcrowding this is causing, prompting the Chief Inspector of Prisons to say:

> My gut feeling is that if we had a proper system of community punishments and community sanctions which were credible, then one third of prisoners need not go to prison. Prison has a role to perform and if you swamp it with people so that it can't do what it is there to do, it is actually not performing as it should. Overcrowding is not just too many people to go in all the cells. It swamps all the work of the education and offending behaviour programmes. Overcrowding means that far too many people are left sitting idle. (Sir David Ramsbottom, Chief Inspector of Prisons)

The single exception to this trend for prisons to become overcrowded, explosive containers is Grendon Underwood, a therapeutic prison which opened in 1962 based on psychological principles. Here, prison wings are run democratically, prisoners are treated humanely, and prison officers work with psychologists to empower prisoners to confront their offending problems. There is a waiting list of prisoners who would like to be transferred to Grendon, and its reoffending rates are lower than any other prison. While treatment programmes designed and delivered by psychologists are at last expanding in UK prisons, it remains a mystery why the successes of Grendon have not been replicated elsewhere.

TREATMENT PROGRAMMES

During the 1970s an influential paper concluded, after surveying the outcomes of a range of intervention strategies with offenders, that:

> with few and isolated exceptions, the rehabilitative efforts that have been reported so far have had no appreciable effect on recidivism. (Martinson, p.33)

This became known as the 'nothing works' thesis which effectively denounced all previous attempts to treat offenders, arguing instead that reoffending has more to do with peer pressure, opportunity, or lack of support than with personal problems. This view particularly appealed to right-wing politicians who favoured 'get tough' policies and knew this would gain them the popular vote. Despite criticisms of Martinson's conclusions and subsequent research demonstrating both the ineffectiveness of incarceration and the potential of treatment programmes (including Martinson, 1979), it has taken some time to discredit the 'nothing works' perspective and to accept that most treatments are better than no treatment at all (Quinsey *et al.*, 1998).

Psychologists have made a significant contribution to the development of effective offender rehabilitation programmes, many of them based on cognitive-behavioural principles (see Hollin, 2000; Bernfield, Farrington and Leschied, 2001). A recent Home Office Research study concludes that:

> Programmes which seek to modify offenders' patterns of thinking and behaving are generally more successful than techniques such as group or individual counselling and non-directive therapy. (Home Office Research Study 171, 1997, p.vii)

Andrews *et al.* (1990) suggest that characteristics of successful treatment programmes will include adequate resources, trained staff who use authority in a 'firm but fair' fashion and who model anti-criminal values, a supportive setting, and a high degree of structure. The programme itself will be matched to offender characteristics, and will target known attitudes and beliefs which encourage criminal behaviour, using a problem-solving approach based on cognitive and social learning principles.

Targeting specific groups of offenders can increase the effectiveness of treatment programmes, and two of the most well-established specialist programmes are **anger management** and sex offender groups. Working in groups is seen as effective since it is not only economical but allows

• **Figure 8.1** A group counselling session

opportunities for sharing experience and rehearsal of coping strategies in a safe but not uncritical environment.

anger management groups

Some of the most critical areas for intervention in relation to young offenders are those of anger and aggression. Problems in these areas can interfere with schooling, family and peer relationships, and may propel adolescents into an escalating spiral in which they lose control and become enmeshed in a pattern of behaviour from which they feel unable to escape. Aggression seems to loom large in the lives of adolescents, especially young men. This may be because of a need to establish an adult masculine identity or uncertainty about the future. Insecurity may result in over-compensation which then reveals itself in aggressive words or posturing behaviour.

Novaco (1975) stressed that anger is not necessarily all bad – we all experience it, and it can serve a useful function, not least in alerting us and others to the possibility of anger turning into aggression. Thus the objective of any treatment targeting anger is effective control and management of the emotion in order to enable the individual to achieve their objectives successfully (see Glick and Goldstein, 1987).

The route by which Novaco suggests anger can be managed is through the acquisition of strategies of self-control; techniques which will allow the individual to deal with a potentially violent situation without becoming aggressive and without losing face. Paradoxically, assertiveness training can ensure that anger is used in a controlled way, while the use of 'stress innoculation' ensures that the individual is exposed to small doses of provocation in such a way that they can develop and practise the necessary skills to cope with such situations in real life. Tackling these situations within a group of peers not only provides authenticity, but can prove an effective reinforcer for the transfer of newly acquired skills into other situations too.

Anger Management Programmes

A typical anger management programme would consist of three stages:

- *cognitive preparation* during which group members are helped to recognise their own personal and physiological anger patterns by carefully analysing previous incidents in which they have lost their temper while also identifying the long-term negative consequences.

- *skill acquisition* when group members learn a range of behavioural and cognitive coping skills which they can employ to deal more effectively with anger-provoking situations, for example relaxation training, assertiveness training, thought-stopping, and self-instructional techniques.

- *application practice* which initially involves role play, but then gradual exposure to potentially anger-provoking situations so that anger control skills can be applied, refined and reinforced. (see *McGuire, 2001*).

These techniques have also been used successfully in relation to older offenders and domestic violence. Dobash *et al.* (1996) found that only 33% of offenders committed further violent acts against their partner in the 12 months following participation in a treatment programme, compared to 75% of offenders who had received an alternative sentence.

Sex offender groups

Marshall, Eccles and Barbaree (1993) have argued that 'sex offenders represent a class of criminals whose crimes call for both punishment and treatment' (p.442). This is because despite support for the treatment of sex offenders, the seriousness of their offences is seen to militate against sentences which have no obvious element of punishment (Brown, 1999). Consequently there is a national programme of sex offender treatment programmes operating in most prisons (SOTP), and the majority of probation services offer similar programmes in the community.

The most common approach used in these programmes is **cognitive-behavioural therapy** which focuses on identifying sexual assault cycles, correcting distorted thinking patterns (for example denial and minimisation), controlling deviant fantasies, increasing empathy for victims, increasing social competencies, and developing relapse prevention skills.

Effective and comprehensive assessment of sex offenders is vital before treatment can begin and will cover social, cognitive, affective, and physiological levels of functioning. Initial interviews will involve systematic analysis of the events surrounding the offence, such as the element of planning, the role of disinhibitors such as drugs or alcohol, the nature and severity of the assault, and the offender's feelings about the victim. The precise nature of the sexual assault cycle can thus be identified. A full social and sexual history will also be taken, which will include details of early family relationships, the frequency and type of sexual activity and fantasy. Personality measures may also be taken, levels of social competence assessed, and cognitive style explored, e.g. the prevalence of distorted beliefs about children or women.

One of the most difficult aspects of this early assessment is coping with denial. Most sex offenders will either totally or partially deny their offences, minimising their role in the offences, and the interviewer may need to use a range of strategies to confront their denial. The most effective include emphasising the positive potential of truthfulness, and using assumptive questioning where, for instance, the offender is asked *when* he committed the offence rather than *if* he did (see Towl and Crighton, 1996).

In terms of the content of treatment programmes, Prentky (1995) provides a useful summary of the target areas for treatment together with strategies for dealing with each of these areas:

• *Correcting distorted thinking patterns*
Most sex offenders justify their behaviour by the use of cognitive distortions, or irrational ideas, which minimise the degree of force used during the offence, the impact on their victims, their role in the offence, or the inappropriateness of their behaviour (see Hatch-Maillette *et al.*, 2001). Since these cognitive distortions tend to be learned attitudes, supported by societal and cultural systems which perpetuate misogyny (hatred of women) and the exploitation of children, they have to be confronted and challenged in a systematic way known as cognitive restructuring. This involves providing accurate information about sexual abuse and its consequences, and helping to reveal the functional role of distorted attitudes, how they allow the offender to avoid responsibility and facing up to his actions. It also includes creating discomfort in the offender by emphasising the victim's distressed response to abuse – their shame, fear, pain and humiliation – in an attempt to help the offender 'own' his behaviour and its dreadful consequences rather than hiding behind convenient cognitive distortions.

Theme link to Perspectives and Issues (**cognitive psychology**)

Many clinical disorders are considered to be disorders of thought and feeling which then lead to inappropriate behaviour. Cognitive psychology has provided a framework for the development of cognitive therapies which aim to challenge and change the pattern of dysfunctional thinking. Therapies which fall into this category include rational–emotive therapy (Ellis, 1973), self-instructional training (Meichenbaum, 1977), and the treatment of automatic thoughts (Beck, 1963).

• *Controlling deviant fantasies*
There is a clear link between deviant sexual fantasy and deviant sexual arousal which may lead to inappropriate and unacceptable behaviour. Sexual arousal is usually measured using an instrument called a plethysmograph which measures penile volume changes in response to a range of auditory and visual

stimuli. This provides a baseline against which to assess changes in arousal which follow treatment. Once a pattern of deviant sexual arousal has been identified, for example to photographs of children, then behavioural techniques which rely on the principles of classical and operant conditioning can be employed either to decrease deviant arousal or to increase the probability of more appropriate arousal.

Theme link to Ethics

Aversion therapy is used to reduce a particular response to a specific stimulus using the principles of classical conditioning. For example, alcoholics are sometimes treated by pairing the use of alcohol with an emetic drug (which causes nausea) so that feelings of nausea become a conditioned response to alcohol. Covert sensitisation is a variation of aversion therapy where patients are asked to imagine the behaviour which needs to be eliminated and then imagine nausea so that the two feelings become associated. In the 1960s aversion therapy was used in an attempt to 'cure' homosexuality, an approach which would be deemed unethical and inappropriate today.

- *Increasing victim empathy*

A lack of empathic concern for victims is a significant feature of all interpersonal violence. Thus, providing offenders with the opportunity to develop empathy may enable them to recognise the pain their victims will suffer and then desist from hurting them. This can be accomplished by exposing offenders to videos of victims describing their feelings and experiences following abuse, enabling them to visualise themselves in a similar situation of betrayal and violation, role play and role reversal taking the role of their victim, and writing letters of apology to their victim (which will not be sent). Many offenders will themselves have experienced victimization as children but may need help to develop more affective appreciation, in order to generalize these feelings towards their own victims. Pithers believes that developing empathy is crucial in treatment programmes for sex offenders:

If empathy can be established, significant effects may be observed in sexual arousal, cognitive distortions, intimacy within interpersonal relationships, realistic self-esteem, and motivation to change and maintain change. (1993, p.190)

Establishing empathy with victims is a vital part of early treatment because it signficantly shifts perception so that denial of pain becomes impossible. The offender can then be assisted to resist the urge towards denial.

• *Improving social competence*

It is recognised that many paedophiles lack competence in their social and interpersonal skills, feeling awkward with adults and much more comfortable with children. Addressing this via **social skills training**, sex education, self-esteem enhancement, relaxation training, and assertiveness training may help such individuals improve their interpersonal relationships with adults, though they may need substantial rehearsal opportunities and positive feedback.

Theme link to Perspectives and Issues **developmental psychology**

Within developmental psychology the role of modelling to shape behaviour emerged from social learning theory (Bandura, 1973). It is a technique for teaching children appropriate behaviour by encouraging them to watch role models displaying the desired behaviour, and rewarding their imitation of this behaviour. The technique can be adapted for adolescents and adults by providing opportunities to imitate the modelled behaviour.

EVALUATION — HOW DO WE KNOW WHEN TREATMENT PROGRAMMES ARE SUCCESSFUL?

Some therapists will argue that any treatment of sex offenders is better than none since no form of treatment makes offenders *more* deviant (Laws, 1985). However, evaluating the success of treatment programmes is particularly difficult because of the under-reporting of offences (by victims and offenders) and the time-scale necessary to be sure of effective rehabilitation. Dwyer and Myers (1990) report a ten-year follow-up of a particular group of sex offenders who volunteered to undergo a particularly comprehensive treatment programme. Recidivism was below 4%, although over two-thirds of the offenders reported experiencing urges to reoffend. When comparing untreated sex offenders with treated sex offenders Marshall *et al.* (1991) claim that 20-60% of untreated offenders reoffend in the five years following release from prison, whereas typically only 15% of treated offenders repeat their offences. One of the problems with evaluation which is solely dependent on reconviction rates, however, is that the rate of reconviction for sexual offences generally is quite low. Levels of sex offending are not falling, but the probability of a reported sexual offence leading to a conviction has significantly declined, for example the conviction rate for rape is only 9%. Thus, demonstrating that a treatment programme has worked by producing a significantly lower reconviction rate becomes problematic, and Friendship and Thornton (2001) suggest that alternative evaluation measures must be considered.

In the UK, evaluation of sex offender programmes has taken place in relation to community programmes and prison programmes. Beckett, Beech, Fisher and Fordham (1994) used what has become known as the STEP method to evaluate community programmes, using pre- and post-psychological measures involving offence-specific and personality assessment techniques, and found that 54% of the offenders in their sample had profiles after treatment which fell within a non-offending range. The same team concluded from their study of prison programmes that two-thirds of the offenders in their sample were successfully treated with regard to offending attitudes, and that longer programmes were more effective than shorter ones (Beech, Fisher & Beckett, 1999).

Crime prevention

It is not simply a truism to say that the most effective way of preventing crime is to decriminalize particular offences, e.g. when sex between consenting adult males in private became legal in 1967 this offence disappeared overnight, though some of the prejudices remain. However, criminal behaviour is extremely diverse, and therefore strategies for preventing crime need to be equally diverse and innovative. A recent Home Office Research Study (1998) suggested that the aims of crime prevention should be to promote a less criminal society, to prevent crime in the community, and to use effective criminal justice interventions. There are four broad approaches to crime prevention which incorporate these aims:

- *primary or developmental prevention* which attempts to reduce the opportunity for crime developing in the individual
- *secondary prevention* which tries to prevent the continuing development of criminality, targeting individuals who may be vulnerable because they have already committed an offence
- *tertiary prevention* which focuses on chronic offenders, offering treatment in an attempt to prevent a return to crime
- *situational or environmental crime prevention* which attempts to reduce opportunities for crime in the environment.

PRIMARY PREVENTION

Within this approach energies are directed towards preventing the onset of criminality, and known risk factors associated with childhood anti-social behaviour have been identified. These include poverty and poor housing; poor parenting; association with delinquent peers, siblings and partners; low intelligence; poor school performance and truancy; high levels of impulsiveness and hyperactivity; and being brought up by a criminal parent (Farrington, 1996). Children who are exposed to multiple risks are disproportionately likely to become serious or persistent offenders.

It is this group of children who need to be targeted, and evaluation of intervention strategies suggests that ineffective strategies include individual casework, counselling, corporal punishment, school suspension, information campaigns and fear arousal (Gottfredson, 1997). Those strategies which do seem to produce success are:

- early home visits and preschool education programmes
- parenting programmes
- family–school initiatives
- anti-bullying strategies in schools.

Utting (1996) provides accounts of 30 such programmes operating in the UK, such as 'Sure Start' and 'On Track'.

There is certainly evidence that early intervention at the preschool or initial school level seems to be successful, whether the focus is on the children (providing training in social-cognitive skills in order to reduce impulsivity) or on parental training to encourage more effective attachment (Hawkins *et al.* 1987). The best known preschool intervention is 'Operation Headstart' which was introduced in America in the 1960s and attempted to accelerate cognitive development in children from high-risk families before their entry to school. Although the evidence for sustained cognitive gains is limited, what these children did seem to gain was enhanced social competence, including reduced aggression and the ability to defer gratification (Zigler and Hall, 1987).

Farrington (2001) suggests that:

Logically, it must be better to prevent offending by intervening early in life than to wait until someone has committed many offences and then intervene – many victims will be spared. And yet most crime reduction resources are devoted to the police, court, prison and probation services and very few to prevention. (p.182)

What is recommended is the setting up of a national agency with a primary mandate for the early prevention of offending, funding and co-ordinating the activities of local agencies while establishing an ongoing cost–benefit analysis of research and practice in the prevention of crime. Farrington suggests that prevention programmes should aim not only to tackle risk factors but also to strengthen protective factors.

SECONDARY PREVENTION

Here the intervention occurs when an individual is showing some signs of antisocial behaviour and has already committed a single or minor offence. The aim is to minimise legal intervention in recognition of the fact that being 'processed' and labelled within the criminal justice system is likely to increase the development of a criminal identity and the probability of further offending. In these cases an informal warning or caution from the police will be given together with a possible referral to the local Juvenile Liaison Bureau, where an interdisciplinary team will work with the young person and their family to identify and resolve recurring problems.

There is also the concept of **restorative justice** which emphasises the value of 'reintegrative shaming' of early offenders – focusing on the offence rather than the offender but requiring the offender to apologise for their actions and make reparation (Braithwaite, 1989). This involves diverting offenders from court and involving them in a process whereby they quite literally make reparation to their victims by apologising and offering some financial compensation or even repairing the damage done. The rationale behind such schemes is that offenders have to reflect on their actions and the consequences of those actions, accepting responsibility and facing their victim while trying to make amends. While it may sound exceedingly simple it is clear that not only is such a scheme inexpensive, but it can be very effective in terms of reducing recidivism and also in helping the victims of crime. Evaluation of such a scheme operating in Northamptonshire has been very favourable, with an estimated cost of £720 per case, in comparison to the cost of £2500 if offenders were taken to court, and a 35% re-offending rate by comparison with 67% (Audit Commission, 1996).

TERTIARY PREVENTION

Providing appropriate treatment programmes for chronic and serious offenders falls into this category. However, harsher forms of tertiary prevention include selective incarceration – keeping high-risk offenders out of circulation altogether, as has been suggested in relation to serious sex offenders and repeat offenders; or severe intervention for young offenders in the form of military-style training, such as 'boot camps' and 'secure training centres'. While there may be instinctive public appeal in some of these options there are no guarantees of success, and serious reservations in terms of human rights. Not all high-risk offenders are correctly classified, and the removal of criminally active individuals from the street may well simply open up criminal opportunities for others eager to step into their shoes.

Recent government proposals to incarcerate indefinitely those deemed to be Dangerous Severe Personality Disordered (DSPN) may also give cause for concern. DPSN is not a clinical diagnosis but is intended to apply to those individuals who pose a risk to the public, even though they may not have committed a criminal offence. While the protection of the public is important there must also be serious consideration of civil liberties.

SITUATIONAL OR ENVIRONMENTAL CRIME PREVENTION

This approach takes a radical move away from the individual and examines the role of the environment in crime, the assumption being that changing the environment can reduce opportunities for crime.

Situational crime prevention takes the following forms:

- **target hardening**
  e.g strengthening coin boxes in telephone kiosks, fitting steering column locks, installing anti-robbery screens in banks.
- **controlling access to crime targets**
  e.g installing entry phones, appointing caretakers, using fencing.
- **surveillance**
  e.g installing Closed Circuit Television (CCTV) and burglar alarms, providing better street lighting.
- **target removal**
  e.g installing removeable car radiios, setting up Women's Refuges, accepting credit cards rather than cash, organising secure late night transport.
- **property identification**
  e.g marking property, vehicle licensing.
- **reducing temptation**
  e.g introducing gender-neutral telephone listings, off-street parking.
- **alerting consciences**
  e.g installing roadside cameras, posting notices alerting people to crime and the role they can play in reducing it.
- **controlling factors which undermine constraint**
  e.g banning alcohol consumption from public places, imposing age checks in premises selling alcohol.
- **making compliance easier**
  e.g introducing more litter bins.

(see Home Office Research Study 187, 1998)

While the results of these types of intervention can look quite impressive, there have been criticisms. They can be costly, and reducing criminal opportunities in one area may result in displacement, whereby criminals turn their attention to other types of crime or other areas. Pease (1994), however, feels this view may be a little pessimistic, especially since introducing crime prevention techniques in specific communities may also provide much-valued protection in those areas particularly beset by crime. The pattern of crime ensures that some areas are signficantly more at risk than others, and it is there that

• **Figure 8.2:** Neighbourhood watch in Wandsworth, London

attention needs to be focused in an attempt to discover what factors make an area more vulnerable.

Another effective form of situational crime prevention involves the community taking action to protect itself. The introduction of neighbourhood watch schemes has proved popular, and Mayhew, Elliott and Dowds (1989) describe such schemes as:

> [having] made more of an impact, in terms of visibility if nothing else, than any other community crime prevention effort in Britain (p.51).

Members of these schemes are encouraged and supported by the police to keep an eye out for any suspicious activity in their community, and to inform the authorities if they do see anything untoward. This activity is very much seen as a partnership with the police, as evidenced by the advertising slogan 'Crime – together we'll crack it'. The effectiveness of neighbourhood watch schemes, however, seems to lie more in the fostering of community spirit and reducing fear of crime rather than in reducing crime itself (Brantingham and Brantingham, 1990). There is a danger of an over-zealous commitment to community protection which can lead to vigilantism, particularly true in areas where communities have wanted to get rid of prostitution, or known sex offenders.

Probably the most well known example of situational crime prevention involves architectural design and environmental psychology. Most environmental approaches to crime prevention rely very much on the principle of informal social controls operating in cohesive communities, and the idea that environmental design can help to encourage a sense of cohesion. According to Newman (1972) crime can be reduced by designing the built environment in such a way as to increase '**defensible space**', or areas for which residents feel some sort of ownership. He pointed out that in many public housing projects, such as high-rise blocks of flats, there are large areas which no-one owns or controls. Because nobody takes responsibility for maintaining these areas they can become magnets for criminal activity. The general effect is a reduction of community activity because people are afraid, and a consequent deterioration in the quality of life.

Theme link to Perspectives and Issues
(applying psychology to everyday life)

Newman (1972) suggested that three environmental features contribute to defensible space:

- **zones of territorial influence**
The notion that if people perceive certain areas as their own space they will take pride in them and defend them is based on ethological theories of territoriality. Additionally, a community which has a shared sense of territoriality is more likely to repel intruders as they will feel uncomfortable and exposed. Architectural design can take account of this by establishing real or symbolic barriers, for example fencing, which should encourage territoriality.

- **opportunities for surveillance**
If buildings are designed in such a way as to allow residents to naturally observe areas, and to recognise outsiders, then it is more likely that offences will be noticed early and reported.

- **image and mileu**
The design of buildings conveys a visual image and an identity, as does the setting. For instance, high-rise blocks all look the same, whereas signs of individuality tend to signal a private area. Similarly a vandalised area can convey disorder and apathy.

In relation to house burglaries, Brown and Altman (1983) suggest the use of three features which can help deter burglars in addition to the normal security measures – barriers, markers and traces. Barriers can be fences, hedges, walls and gates, while markers and traces include indications of occupation, e.g. house name plates, and garden furniture. Garages also help prevent burglaries because they make it hard for potential burglars to know whether anyone is home.

The concept of **zero tolerance** gained increasing significance in the 1990s and is a strategy based on the principle that acting swiftly against small crimes helps reduce the bigger ones too. It stems from the work of Wilson and Kelling (1982) who argued that allowing a climate of disorder to develop leads to more serious crimes, so for instance leaving a broken window in a building and not repairing it will inspire some individuals to vandalise the rest of the building. From small beginnings, these vandals may turn to more serious crimes.

> A piece of property is abandoned, weeds grow up, a window is smashed … Adults stop scolding rowdy children; the children, emboldened, become more rowdy. Families move out … many residents will think that crime, especially violent crime, is on the rise, and they will modify their behavior accordingly. They will use the streets less often, and when on the streets will stay apart from their fellows … It is more likely that here, rather than in places where people are confident they can regulate behaviour by informal controls, drugs will change hands, prostitutes will solicit, and cars will be stripped. (Wilson and Kelling, p.30)

Particular concern was expressed about specific communities becoming 'no-go areas' for the police. Introducing hard-edged policing was seen as a way of helping the law-abiding people in these communities to regain control. Thus the problems of noise, graffitti, rowdy behaviour and disruptive neighbours were to be addressed head on.

Policies of zero tolerance in America appeared at one level to be effective, in that reported crime decreased in most major cities, and the concept was wholeheartedly embraced by the British government. However, the crime figures declined simultaneously in areas where zero tolerance policies were practised and where they were not. Many criminologists pointed out that the reasons for the decline were more likely to be the result of intensified police efforts and increased resources, together with increased numbers of offenders being sent to prison. Caution is therefore advised in relation to zero tolerance policies since over-zealous implementation can damage police–community relations (Kelling and Coles, 1996).

Summary

It is clear that some approaches to treating offenders and reducing crime are effective and others are not. Targeting specific groups of offenders, such as sex offenders, and designing treatment programmes based on cognitive–behavioural principles, appears to reduce reoffending rates. Similarly, targeting specific high-risk communities with appropriate strategies for reducing crime has the benefit of restoring control to these communities and reducing repeat victimization. For a crime reduction strategy to work it needs co-operation from a variety of agencies, and the contribution of psychologists to the design, implementation and evaluation of such a strategy is crucial.

KEY TERMS

reconviction rates
recidivism
rehabilitation
cognitive–behavioural treatment
programmes
anger-management
social skills training
restorative justice
situational/environmental crime
prevention
defensible space
zero tolerance

EXERCISE **1**

The treatment of sex offenders is controversial. Many would argue that this group of offenders perhaps more than any other deserves punishment, and that the offer of treatment while they are in prison is pointless since they clearly do not wish or are unable to change their behaviour. Moreover they may opt for treatment quite cynically in order to secure earlier release or less intrusive supervision in the community. Perkins (1990), however, strongly argues the case for treating sex offenders on the following grounds:

- treatment may enable sex offenders to modify their behaviour, while no treatment clearly will effect no change.
- treatment may counteract the negative influences of

imprisonment, e.g. confined contact with other sex offenders which might lead to a strengthening of sexual deviation, and long periods of incarceration which may further impair offenders' social competence.

- treatment may enable researchers to build up a body of knowledge which might help to reduce the possibility of sexual offences.
- treatment may be entirely appropriate for those individuals whose offending could be related to their own sexual victimization as children.
- where sexual abuse has occurred within a family setting and there is a possiblity of reintegration, treatment will be essential.

Split into two groups, with one group constructing a series of arguments which a newspaper like the *News of the World* might present to support the idea of incarcerating sex offenders and throwing away the key. The other group should compose a letter to the editor outlining why they think treatment programmes should be funded.

EXERCISE **2**

Construct a scale which measures attitudes to crime (such that a high score indicates high fear of crime), and then give this scale to three groups of people. For each group show them a photo first: Group 1 could be shown a photo of an abandoned and damaged car, Group 2 could be shown a photo of an affluent neighbourhood, and Group 3 could be shown a photograph of a police officer. How do you think the attitudes of these three groups might differ? What theories of crime reduction influence this type of investigation?

EXERCISE **3**

Think of a scenario which might be used in an anger management programme for young men, for example having a drink spilled over a girlfriend. List their likely reactions to this event (thoughts and behaviour), and the possible alternatives, bearing in mind the contribution of cognitive and social psychology to the processes you will be considering.

Recommended reading and web sites

Ainsworth, P.B. (2001) *Offender Profiling and Crime Analysis*. Cullompton: Willan Publishing.

Ainsworth, P.B. (2000) *Psychology and Crime: Myths and Reality*. Harlow: Longman.

Blackburn, R. (1993) *The Psychology of Criminal Conduct*. Chichester: Wiley.

Hollin, C. (ed) (2000) *Handbook of Offender Assesment and Treatment*. Chichester: Wiley.

Hughes, G. (1998) *Crime Prevention*. Buckingham: Open University Press.

Jackson, J.L. & Bekarian, D.A. (eds) (1997) *Offender Profiling: Theory, Research and Practice*. Chichester: Wiley.

Maguire, M., Morgan, R. & Reiner, R. (eds) (1997) *The Oxford Handbook of Criminology*, 2nd ed. London: Oxford University Press.

Vold, G.B., Bernard, T.J. & Snipes, J.B. (1998) *Theoretical Criminology*. Oxford: Oxford University Press.

Wrightsman, L.S. (2001) *Forensic Psychology*. Belmont, CA: Wadsworth.

There are lots of sites on the internet which will provide information about forensic psychology, crime, and criminal statistics. Some of these are:

http://www.homeoffice.gov.uk/

http://mitretek.org/justice/cjlinks/

http://www.oklahoma.net/~jnichols/forensic.html

http://www.kcl.ac.uk/ccjs

http://www.le.ack.uk/cp/cp.html

http://www.sps.gov.uk

http://www.aic.gov.au

http://www.ncjrs.org

http://www.nicic.org

http://psych-server.iastate.edu/faculty/gwells/guidelines.html

http://www.crimelibrary.com

http://www.usfca.edu/pj/camera-mason.htm

Be very wary about other sites, unless they are associated with an academic institution – you can tell UK universities because they have **ac.uk** in their site title, US universities because they have **edu** in their site title, and government sites because they have **gov** in their site title. If you are going to be using any internet information in your coursework you need to use the proper citation so the site can be checked (see http://apa.org/journal/webref.html for referencing advice).

References

Ainsworth, P.B. (1995) *Psychology and Policing in a Changing World*. Chichester: Wiley.

Ainsworth, P.B. (1995) *Turning heroes into villains: The role unconscious transference in media crime reporting.* Paper presented at the 5th European Conference on Law and Psychology, Budapest.

Ainsworth, P.B. (2000) *Psychology and Crime: Myths and Reality*. Harlow: Pearson.

Andrews, D.A., Zinger, I., Hoge, R.D., Bonta, J., Gendreau, P. & Cullen, F.T. (1990) Does correctional treatment work? A clinically relevant and psychologically informed meta-analysis. *Criminology*. 28, 369–404.

Ashton, J., Brown, I., Senior, B. & Pease, K. (1998) Repeat victimisation: Offender accounts. *International Journal of Risk, Security and Crime Prevention*.

Badcock, R. (1997) Developmental and clinical issues in relation to offending in the individual. In J.L. Jackson and D.A. Bekerian (eds) *Offender Profiling: Theory, Research and Practice.* Chichester: Wiley.

Bagby, R.M., Parker, J.D., Rector, N.A. & Kalemba, V. (1994) Racial prejudice in the Canadian legal system: Juror decisions in a simulated rape trial. *Law and Human Behavior.* 18, 339–350.

Baldwin, J. & McConville, M. (1980) Juries, foremen and verdicts. *British Journal of Criminology*. 20, 35–44.

Baldwin, J. (1993) Police interview techniques: Establishing truth or proof. *British Journal of Criminology*. 33, 325–352.

Bandura, A. (1973) *Aggression: A social learning analysis*. London: Prentice Hall.

Bandura, A. (1977) *Social Learning Theory*. Eaglewood Cliffs: Prentice Hall.

Bartlett, F.C. (1932) *Remembering*. Cambridge: Cambridge University Press.

Bartol, C.R. & Bartol, A.M. (1999) History of Forensic Psychology. In A.K. Hess & I.B. Weiner (eds) *Handbook of Forensic Psychology*. New York: John Wiley.

Beck, A.T. (1963) Thinking and depression. *Archives of General Psychiatry*. 9, 324–333.

Beckett, R., Beech, A., Fisher, D. & Fordham, A.S (1994) *Community-based treatment for sex offenders: An evaluation of seven treatment programmes.* London: Home Office Publishers.

Bee, H. (1995) *The Developing Child*. New York: Harper Collins.

Beech, A., Fisher, D. & Beckett, R. (1999) *An evaluation of the Prison Sex Offender Treatment Programme*. London: Home Office Publishers.

Bernfield, G., Farrington, D. & Leschied, A. (2001) *Offender Rehabilitation in Practice*. Chichester: Wiley.

Blackburn, R. (1993) *The Psychology of Criminal Conduct*. Chichester: Wiley.

Bohman, M. (1996) Predisposition to criminality: Swedish adoption studies in retrospect. In G.R. Bock & J.A. Goode (eds) *Genetics of criminal and antisocial behaviour* (Ciba Foundation Symposium 194) (pp. 99–114) Chichester: Wiley.

Bouchard, T.J., Lykken, D.T., McGue, M., Segal, N.L. & Tellegen, A. (1990) Sources of hyman psychological differences: The Minneapolis study of twins reared apart. *Science*. 250, 223–228.

Bowlby, J. (1944) Forty-four juvenile theives. *International Journal of Psychoanalysis*. 25, 1–57.

Braithwaite, J. (1989) *Crime, Shame and Reintegration*. New York: Cambridge University Press.

Brantingham, P.L. & Brantingham, P.J. (1990) Situational Crime Prevention in Practice. *Canadian Journal of Criminology*. 32, 17–40.

Brown, B.A. & Altman, I. (1983) Territoriality, defensible space, and residential burglary: An environmental analysis. *Journal of Environmental Psychology*. 3, 203–220.

Brown, J. (1998) Helping the police with their inquiries. *The Psychologist*. November, 539–542.

Brown, L. & Willis, A. (1985) Authoritarianism in British police recruits: Importation, socialisation or myth? *Journal of Occupational Psychology*. 58, 97–108.

Brown, R. & Kulik, J. (1977) Flashbulb memories. *Cognition*. 5, 73–79.

Brown, S. (1999) Public attitudes towards the treatment of sex offenders. *Legal and Criminological Psychology*. 4, 239–252.

Bruck, M. & Ceci, S.J. (1995) Amicus brief for the case of New Jersey v. Margaret Kelly Michaels. *Psychology, Public Policy and Law*. 1, 272–322.

Brussel, J.A. (1968) *Casebook of a Crime Psychiatrist*. New York: Simon & Schuster.

Bull, R. & McAlpine, S. (1998) Facial Appearance and Criminality. In A. Memon, A. Vrij & R. Bull, *Psychology and Law: Truthfulness, accuracy and credibility*. Maidenhead: McGraw-Hill.

Cain, M. (1989) Feminists transgress criminology. In M. Cain (ed) *Growing Up*

Good. London: Sage.

Campbell, B. (1993) *Goliath: Britain's dangerous places*. London: Virago Press.

Campbell, C. (1976) Portrait of a mass killer. *Psychology Today*. 9, 110–119.

Canter, D. (1994) *Criminal Shadows: Inside the mind of the serial killer*. London: Harper Collins.

Canter, D. (2000) Offender profiling and criminal differentiation. *Legal and Criminological Psychology*. 5, 23–46.

Canter, D. & Alison, L.J. (1999) *Profiling in Policy and Practice*. Dartmouth: Ashgate.

Carroll, J. & Weaver, F. (1986) Shoplifters' perceptions of crime opportunities: A process-tracing study. In D.B. Cornish & R.V.G. Clarke (eds) *The Reasoning Criminal: Rational choice perspectives on offending*. New York: Springer-Verlag.

Chance, J.E. & Goldstein, A.G. (1996) The other-race effect and eyewitness identification. In S.L. Sporer, R.S. Malpass & G. Koehnken (eds) *Psychological Issues in Eyewitness Identification.* Hillsdale, NJ: Lawrence Erlbaum.

Chess, S. & Thomas, A. (1984) *Origins and Evolution of Behavior Disorders*. New York: Brunner/Mazel.

Chodorow, N. (1978) *The Reproduction of Mothering*. Berkeley, CA: University of California Press.

Christiansen, K.O. (1977) A preliminary study of criminality among twins. In S. Mednick & K.O. Christiansen (eds) *Biological Bases of Criminal Behavior*. New York: Gardner Press.

Christianson, S.A. (1992) Emotional stress and eyewitness memory: A critical review. *Psychological Bulletin*. 112, 284–309.

Clarke, A.M. & Clarke, A.D.B. (1998) Early experience and the life path. *The Psychologist*. 11 (9), 433–436.

Clifford, B.R. (1993) Witnessing: A comparison of adults and children. *Issues in Criminological and Legal Psychology*. 20, 15–21.

Coleman, C., & Moynihan, J. (1996). *Understanding crime data: Haunted by the dark figure*. Buckingham: Open University Press.

Copson, G. (1995) *Coals to Newcastle? Part 1: A Study of Offender Profiling* (Paper 7) London: Police Research Group Special Interest Series, Home Office.

Copson, G. & Holloway, K. (1997) *Offender Profiling*. Paper presented to the Annual Conference of the British Psychological Society's Division of Criminological and Legal Psychology, Cambridge, England.

Cornish, D.B. & Clark, R.V. (eds) (1986) *The Reasoning Criminal: Rational choice perspectives on offending*. New York: Springer-Verlag.

Cortes, J.B. & Gatti, F.M. (1972) *Delinquency and Crime: A biopsychosocial approach*. New York: Seminar Press.

Crawford, A. (1998) *Crime Prevention and Community Safety: Politics, policies* and practices. Harlow: Longman.

Crombag, H.F.M., Wagenaar, W.A. & Van Kopen, P.J. (1996) Crashing memories and the problem of source monitoring. *Applied Cognitive Psychology.* 10, 95–104.

Crowe, R.R. (1974) An adoption study of antisocial personality. *Archives of General Psychiatry.* 31, 785–791.

Cutler, B.L. & Penrod, S.D. (1995) *Mistaken Identification: The eyewitness, psychology and the law*. New York; Cambridge University Press.

Dale, A. (1997) Modelling criminal offences. *The Police Journal* LXX (2), April, 104–116.

Davies, G.M. & Noon, E. (1991) *An evaluation of the live link for child witnesses*. London: Home Office.

Davies, G.M. (1992) Influencing public policy on eyewitnessing: Problems and possibilities. In F. Losel, D.Bender & T.Bleisener (eds) *Psychology and Law: International Perspectives.* New York: Walter de Gruyter.

Deosoran, R. (1993) The social psychology of selecting jury forepersons. *British Journal of Psychology.* 33, 70–80.

DeSantis, A. & Kayson, W.A. (1997) Defendants' characteristics of attractiveness, race, and sex, and sentencing decisions. *Psychological Reports.* 81, 2, 679–683.

Dion, K.K., Bersheid, E. & Walster, E. (1972) What is beautiful is good. *Journal of Personality and Social Psychology.* 24, 285–290.

Dobash, R., Dobash, R., Cavanagh, K. & Lewis, J. (1996) *Research evaluation of programmes for violent offenders*. Edinburgh: Scottish Office.

Douglas, J. & Olshaker, M. (1995) *Mindhunter: Inside the FBI Elite Serial Crime Unit*. New York: Scribner.

Downs, A.C. & Lyons, P.M. (1991) Natural observations of the links between attractiveness and initial legal judgements. *Personality and Social Psychology Bulletin.* 17, 541–547.

Duncan, B.L. (1976) Different social perceptions and attribution of intergroup violence: Testing the lower limits of stereotyping of blacks. *Journal of Personality and Social Psychology.* 34, 590–598.

Durkin, K. & Houghton, S. (2000) Children's and adolescents' stereotypes of tattooed people as delinquent. *Legal and Criminological Psychology.* 5, 153–164.

Dwyer, S.M. & Myers, S. (1990) Sex offender treatment: A six-month to ten-year follow up study. *Annals of Sex Research.* 3 (3), 305–318.

Eckensberger, L.H. (1994) Moral development and its measurement across cultures. In W.J. Lonner & R.S. Malpass (eds) *Psychology and Culture.* Boston: Allyn & Bacon.

Ellis, A. (1973) *Humanistic psychotherapy*. New York: McGraw Hill.

Ellsworth, P.C. (1993) Some steps between attitudes and verdicts. In R. Hastie (ed) *Inside the Juror*. New York: Cambridge University Press.

Eron, L.D., Huesmann, L.R. & Zelli, A. (1991) The role of parental variables in the learning of aggression. In D.J. Peplar & H.K. Rubin (eds) *The Development and Treatment of Childhood Aggression*. Hillsdale: Erlbaum.

Eysenck, H.J. (1964) *Crime and Personality*. London: Routledge and Kegan Paul.

Eysenck, H.J. & Gudjonsson, G. (1989) *The Causes and Cures of Criminality*. New York: Plenum Press.

Farrell, G. & Pease, K. (1993) *Once bitten, twice bitten: Repeat victimisation and its implications for crime prevention*. Crime Prevention Unit Paper 46. London: HMSO.

Farrington, D. (1996) *Understanding and preventing youth crime*. York: Joseph Rowntree Foundation.

Farrington, D. (1997) Human development and criminal careers. In M. Maguire, R. Morgan & R. Reiner (eds) *The Oxford Handbook of Criminology*. Oxford: Oxford University Press.

Farrington, D. (2001) Crime Prevention. *The Psychologist*. 14 (4), 182–183.

Feldman, P. (1993) *The Psychology of Crime*. Cambridge: Cambridge University Press.

Few, C. (2001) *Using statement validity analysis in rape allegations*. Paper presented at the British Psychological Society Annual Conference, April, Glasgow.

Fisher, R.P. & Geiselman, R.E. (1992) *Memory enhancing techniques for investigative interviewing*. Springfield, IL: Charles C. Thomas.

Fivush, R. (1993) Developmental perspectives on autobiographical recall. In G.S. Goodman & B.I Bottoms (eds) *Child Victims, Child Witnesses: Understanding and improving testimony.* New York: The Guildford Press.

Forrester, D., Frenz, S., O'Connor, M. & Pease, K. (1990) *The Kirkholt Burglary Prevention Project Phase II.* Crime Prevention Unit Paper 23. London: Home Office.

Friendship, C. & Thornton, D. (2001) Sexual reconviction for sexual offenders discharged from prison in England and Wales: Implications for evaluating treatment. *British Journal of Criminology*. 41, 285–292.

Freedman, J.L, Martin, C.K. & Mota, V.L. (1998) Pre-trial publicity: Effects of admonition and expressing pre-trial opinions. *Legal and Criminological Psychology*. 3, 255–270.

Frosh, S. (1994) *Sexual Difference: Masculinity and psychoanalysis*. London: Routledge.

Furnham, A. & Thompson, J. (1991) Personality and self-reported delinquency. *Personality and Individual Differences*. 12, 585–598.

Geiselman, R.E, Fisher, R.P., Firstenberg, I., Hutton, L.A., Sulliva, S., Artisan, I. & Prosket, A. 91984) Enhancement of eyewitness memory: An empirical evaluation of the cognitive interview. *Journal of Police Science and Administration*. 12, 74–80.

Gilligan, C. (1982) *In a Different Voice: Psychological theory and women's development*. Cambridge, MA: Harvard University Press.

Glueck, S. & Glueck, E.T. (1956) *Physique and Delinquency*. New York: Dodd Meade.

Glick, B. & Goldstein, A.P. (1987) *Aggression Replacement Training*. Champaigne, IL: Research Press.

Godden, D. & Baddeley, A.D. (1975) Context dependent memory in two natural environments: On land and underwater. *British Journal of Psychology*. 66, 325–331.

Goldstein, A.C. & Chance, C. (1971) Visual recognition memory for complex configurations. *Perception and Psychophysics*. 9, 237–241.

Goodey, J. (1997) Boys don't cry: Masculinities, fear of crime and fearlessness. *British Journal of Criminology*. 37 (3), 401–418.

Gordon, D.A. & Arbuthnot, J. (1987) Individual, group and family interventions. In H.C. Quay (ed) *Handbook of Juvenile Delinquency*. New York: Wiley.

Gordon, R.A., Bindrim, T., McNicholas, M. & Walden, T. (1988) Perceptions of blue-collar and white-collar crime: The effect of defendant race on simulated juror decisions. *Journal of Social Psychology*. 128 (2) 191–197.

Gottfredson, D. (1997) School based crime prevention. In L.W. Sherman *et al*. *Preventing Crime: What works, what doesn't, what's promising*. Washington: US Department of Justice.

Gowan, M.A. & Gatewood, R.D. (1995) Personnel Selection. In N. Brewer & C. Wilson (eds) *Psychology and Policing*. Hillsdale, NJ: Lawrence Earlbaum.

Graef, R. (1990) *Talking Blues: The police in their own worlds*. London: Fontana.

Gudjonsson, G. (1992) *The Psychology of Interrogations, Confessions and Testimony*. Chichester: Wiley.

Gudjonsson, G. (1989) Compliance in an interrogation situation: a new scale. *Personality and Individual Differences*. 10, 535–540.

Gudjonsson, G.E & Copson, G. (1997) The role of the expert in criminal investigation. In J.L. Jackson & D.A. Bekarian (eds) *Offender Profiling: Theory, Research and Practice*. Chichester: Wiley.

Haney, C. (1993) Psychology and legal change: The impact of a decade. *Law and Human Behaviour*. 17, 371–398.

Hans, V.P. & Vidmar, N. (1982) Jury Selection, in N.I Kerr & R.M Bray (eds) *The Psychology of the Courtroom*. London: Academic Press.

Hans, V.P. (1992) Jury Decision Making, in D.R. Kagehiro & W.S. Laufer (eds) *Handbook of Psychology and Law*. New York: Springer.

Hargreaves, D.H. (1980) Classrooms, schools and juvenile delinquency. *Educational Analysis*. 2, 75–87.

Harris, J.R. (1998) *The Nurture Assumption: Why children turn out the way they do*. New York: The Free Press.

Harrower, J. (1999) When Children Kill. *Psychology Review*, 6 (2)

Hartl, E.M., Monnelly, E.P. & Elderkin, R. (1982) *Physique and Delinquent Behaviour: A thirty year follow-up of William H. Sheldon's Varieties of Delinquent Youth.* New York: Academic Press.

Hastie, R., Penrod, S.D. & Pennington, N. (1983) *Inside the Jury.* Cambridge, MA: Harvard University Press.

Hastie, R. (ed) (1993) *Inside the Juror.* New York: Cambridge University Press.

Hastorf, A.H. & Cantril, H. (1954) They saw the game: A case study. *Journal of Abnormal and Social Psychology.* 49, 129–134.

Hatch-Maillette, M.A., Scalora, M.J., Huss, M.T. & Baumgartner, J.V. (2001) Criminal Thinking Patterns: Are child molestors unique? *International Journal of Offender Therapy and Comparative Criminology.* 45 (1), 102–117.

Hawkins, J.D., Catalano, R.F., Jones, G. & Fine, D. (1987) Delinquency prevention through parent training: Results and issues from work in progress. In J.Q Wilson & G.C. Loury (eds) *From Children to Citizens: Volume 3: Families, Schools and Deliquency Prevention.* New York: Springer-Verlag.

Healy, D. (1997) *The Antidepressant Era.* New York: Harvard University Press.

Hedderman, C. & Hough, M. (1994) *Does the criminal justice system treat men and women differently?* Research Findings No. 8. London: HMSO.

Heidensohn, F. (1968) The deviance of women: A critique and an enquiry. *British Journal of Sociology.* 19 (2), 160–175.

Heidensohn, F. (1995) Feminist perspectives and their impact on criminology and criminal justice in Britain. In N. Hahn Rafter & F. Heidensohn (eds) *International Feminist Perspectives in Criminology.* Buckingham: Open University Press.

Heider, F. (1958) *The Psychology of Interpersonal Relations.* New York: John Wiley.

Hindelang, M.J. (1979) Sex differences in criminal activity. *Social Problems.* 27, 143–156.

Hirschi, T. (1969) *Causes of Delinquency.* Berkeley, CA: University of California Press.

Hodge, J., McMurran, M. & Hollin, C. (eds) (1997) *Addicted to Crime?* Chichester: John Wiley.

Hollin, C.R. (1992) *Criminal Behaviour.* London: Taylor & Francis.

Hollin, C.R. (2000) (ed) *Handbook of Offender Assesment and Treatment.* Chichester: Wiley.

Holmes, R.M. & Holmes, S.T. (1996) *Profiling Violent Crimes: An investigative tool.* Thousand Oaks, CA: Sage.

Home Office (1992) *Memorandum of Good Practice.* London: HMSO

Home Office Research Study 171 (1997) *Changing Offenders' Attitudes and Behaviour – what works?* London: HMSO

Home Office Research Study 187 (1998) *Reducing Offending: An assessment of research evidence on ways of dealing with offending behaviour*. London: HMSO.

Home Office Section 95 Report (1999) *Statistics on women and the criminal justice system*. London: HMSO.

Home Office Section 95 Report (2000) *Statistics on race and the criminal justice system*. London: HMSO.

Howitt, D. (1998) *Crime, Media and the Law*. Chichester: Wiley.

Jackson, D. (1995) *Destroying the baby in themselves: Why did the two boys kill James Bulger?* Nottingham: Mushroom Publications.

Jackson, J.L. & Bekarian, D.A. (eds) (1997) *Offender Profiling: Theory, Research and Practice.* Chichester: Wiley.

James, W. (1890) *The Principles of Psychology*. New York: Holt.

Jarvik, L.E., Klodin, V. & Matsuyama, S.S. (1973) Human aggression and the extra Y chromosome: Fact or fantasy? *American Psychologist*. 28, 674–682.

Jefferson, T. & Carlen, P. (eds) (1996) Masculinities, social relations and crime. *British Journal of Criminology,* 36 (3).

Johnson, M.K., Hashtroudi, S. & Lindsay, D.S. (1993) Source Monitoring. *Psychological Bulletin*. 114, 3–28.

Jordan, P. (1998) Effective policing strategies for reducing crime. In Home Office Research Study 187 (1998) *Reducing Offending: An assessment of research evidence on ways of dealing with offending behaviour*. London: HMSO.

Kadane, J.B. (1993) Sausages and the law: Juror decisions in the much larger justice system. In R. Hastie (ed) *Inside the Juror*. Cambridge: Cambridge University Press.

Kagehiro (1990) Defining the standard of proof in jury instructions. *Psychological Science*. 1 (3), 194–200.

Kahn, A. (1984) *Victims of Violence: Final Report of APA Task Force on the Victims of Crime and Violence*. Washington: American Psychological Association.

Kalven, H. & Zeisel, H. (1966) *The American Jury*. Chicago: University of Chicago Press.

Katz, J. (1988) *The Seductions of Crime*. New York: Basic Books.

Kegan, R.G. (1986) The child behind the mask: Sociopathy as developmental delay. In W.H. Reid, D. Dorr, J.I. Walker & J.W. Bonner (eds) *Unmasking the Psychopath: Antisocial personality and related syndromes*. London: W.W. Norton.

Kelling, G.L. & Coles, C.M. (1996) *Fixing Broken Windows: Restoring order and reducing crime in the community*. New York: Free Press.

Kerr, N.I. & Bray, R.M. (eds) (1982) *The Psychology of the Courtroom*. London: Academic Press.

Kershaw, C., Budd, T., Kinshott G., Mattinson, J., Mayhew, P. & Myhill, A.

(2000) *The 2000 British Crime Survey*. Home Office Statistical Bulletin, 18/00. London: HMSO.

Kilpatrick, R. (1997) Joy-riding: An addictive behaviour. In J. Hodge, M. McMurran, & C. Hollin (eds) *Addicted to Crime?* Chichester: John Wiley.

Kirsta, A. (1994) *Deadlier than the Male*. London: Harper Collins.

Kocsis, R.N., Irwin, H.J., Hayes, A.F. & Nunn, R. (2000) Expertise in psychological profiling: A comparative assessment. *Journal of Interpersonal Violence*. 15 (3), 311–331.

Kohlberg, L. (1976) Moral stages and moralisation: The cognitive developmental approach. In T. Lickona (ed) *Moral Development and Behavior*. New York: Holt, Rinehart and Winston.

Koluchova, J. (1991) Severely deprived twins after 22 years observation. *Studia Psychologica*. 33, 23–28.

Krauss, S.J. (1995) Attitudes and the prediction of behavior: A meta-analysis of the empirical literature. *Personality and Social Psychology Bulletin*. 21, 58–75.

Langer,W. (1972) *The Mind of Adolf Hitler*. New York: Basic Books.

Laws, D.R. (1985) Sexual fantasy alteration: Procedural considerations. *Journal of Behaviour Therapy and Experimental Psychiatry*. 16 (1), 39–44.

Lerner, M.J. (1970) The desire for justice and reactions to victims. In J. Macauley & L. Berkowitz (eds) *Altruism and Helping Behaviour*. Orlando, Fl: Academic Press.

Liposvky, J.A., Tidwell, R., Crisp, J., Kilpatrick, D.G., Saunders, B.E. & Dawson, V.L. (1992) Child witnesses in criminal courts: Descriptive information from three southern states. *Law and Human Behavior*. 16, 635–650.

Lipsey, M.W. (1992) The effect of treatment on juvenile delinquents: Results from meta-analysis. In Loser, F., Bliesener, T. & Bender, D. (eds) *Psychology and Law: International Perspectives*. Berlin: de Gruyter.

Loftus, E.F. (1974) Reconstructive memory: The incredible eyewitness. *Psychology Today*. 8, 116–119.

Loftus, E.F. (1979) *Eyewitness Testimony*. Cambridge: Harvard University Press.

Loftus, E.F. & Palmer, J.C. (1974) Reconstruction of automobile destruction: An example of the interaction between language and memory. *Journal of Verbal Learning and Verbal Behaviour*. 13, 585–589.

Loftus, E.F. & Zanni, G. (1975) Eyewitness testimony: The influence of the wording of a question. *Bulletin of the Psychonomic Society*. 5, 86–88.

Loftus, E.F. & Ketcham, K.E. (1983) The malleability of eyewitness accounts. In S.M.A. Lloyd-Bostock & B.R. Clifford (eds) *Evaluating Witness Evidence: Recent psychological research and new perspectives*. Chichester: Wiley.

Loftus, E.F., Loftus, G.R. & Messo, J. (1987) Some facts about weapon focus. *Law and Human Behavior*. 11, 55–62.

Lombroso, C. & Ferrero, W. (1895) *The Female Offender*. London: Fisher Unwin.

Lombroso, C. (1911) *Crime: Its causes and remedies*. Boston: Little Brown.

Loohs, S. (1996) *Mnemonic aids in questioning children: Misleading, useless or helpful?* Paper presented to the 6th European Conference on Law and Psychology, Sienna, Italy.

Lupfer, M.B., Doan, K. & Houston, D.A. (1998) Explaining unfair and fair outcomes: The therapeutic value of attributional analysis. *British Journal of Social Psychology*. 37 (4), 495–512.

Maguire, M., Morgan, R. & Reiner, R. (eds) (1997) *The Oxford Handbook of Criminology*. Second edition. London: Oxford University Press.

Mai, R.Y. & Alpert, J.L. (2000) Separation and socialisation: A feminist analysis of the school shootings at Columbine. *Journal for the Psychoanalysis of Culture and Society.* 5 (2), 264–275.

Marshall, W., Ward, T., Jones, R., Johnston, P. & Barbaree, H.E. (1991) An optimistic evaluation of treatment outcome with sex offenders. *Violence Update*, March, 1–8.

Marshall, W. L., Eccles, A. and Barbaree, H. E. (1993) A Three-Tiered Approach to the Rehabilitation of Sex Offenders. *Behavioural Sciences and the Law.* 11, 441–455.

Martinson, R. (1974) What works? Questions and answers about prison reform. *The Public Interest*. 35, 22–54.

Martinson, R. (1979) New findings, new views: A note of caution regarding sentencing reform. *Hostra Law Review*. 7, 242–258.

Masters, F. & Greaves, D. (1969) The Quazimodo Complex. *British Journal of Plastic Surgery*. 20, 204–210.

Marxen, D., Yuille, J.C. & Nisbett, M. (1995) The complexities of eliciting and assessing children's statements. *Psychology, Public Policy, and Law*. 1, 450–460.

Mauet, T.A. & McCrimmon, I.A. (1993) *Fundamentals of Trial Techniques*. Melbourne: Longman.

Mayhew, P.M., Elliott, D. & Dowds, L. (1989) The 1988 British Crime Survey. London: HMSO.

McGuire, J. & Priestley, P. (1985) *Offending Behaviour*. London: Batsford.

McGuire, J. (2001) *Offender Rehabilitation and Treatment*. Chichester: Wiley.

Mears, D.P., Ploeger, M. & Warr, M. (1998) Explaining the gender gap in delinquency: Peer influence and moral evaluations of behaviour. *Journal of Research in Crime and Delinquency.*

Mednick, S.A., Gabrielli, W.F. & Hutchings, B. (1987) Genetic factors in the etiology of criminal behaviour. In S.A. Mednick, T.E. Moffit, & S.S. Stack (eds) *The Causes of Crime*. Cambridge: Cambridge University Press.

Meichenbaum, D. (1977) *Cognitive behaviour modification: An integrative approach*. New York: Plenum.

Memon, A. & Stevenage, S. (1996) Interviewing witnesses: What works and what doesn't? *Psycholoquy*, 96.7.06.witness-memory.1.memon

Memon, A. (1998) Telling it all: The cognitive interview. In A. Memon, A.Vrij & R.Bull (eds) *Psychology and Law: Truthfulness, Accuracy and Credibility.* Maidenhead: McGraw Hill.

Memon, A & Bull, R. (2000) *Handbook of the Psychology of Interviewing.* Chichester: Wiley.

Messerschmidt, J.W. (1993) *Masculinities and Crime*. Lanham: Rowman and Littlefield.

Milgram, S. (1973) *Obedience to Authority*. London: Tavistock.

Milne, R. & Bull, R. (1999*) Investigative Interviewing*. Chichester: Wiley.

Mirlees-Black, C. (1992) *Using Psychometric Personality Tests in the Selection of Firearms Officers*. Home Office Research and Planning Unit Paper 68. London: HMSO.

Mitchell, M. & Munroe, A. (1996) The influence of the occupational culture on how police probationers learn to deal with incidents of sudden death. In N.C. Clark & G.M. Stephenson (eds) *Psychological Perspectives on Police and Custodial Culture and Organisation.* Leicester: British Psychological Society.

Moir, A. & Jessel, D. (1995) *A Mind to Crime*. London: Harper Collins.

Moston, S. Stephenson, G.M. & Williamson, T.M. (1992) The effects of case characteristics on suspect behaviour during police questioning. *British Journal of Criminology*. 32, 23–40.

Newburn, T. & Stanko, E. (eds) (1994) *Just Boys Doing Business: Men, masculinities and crime*. London: Routledge.

Newman, O. (1972) *Defensible Space*. New York: Macmillan.

Novaco, R.W.(1975) *Anger control: The development and evaluation of an experimental treatment*. Lexington: D.C. Heath.

Oakley, A. (1972) *Sex, Gender and Society*. London: Temple Smith.

O'Keefe, C. & Alison, J. (2000) Rhetoric in psychic detection. *Journal for the Society for Psychical Research*. 64 (858), 26–38.

Oleson, J.C.(1996) Psychological profiling: Does it actually work? *Forensic Update*. 46, 11–14.

Osborn, S.G. & West, D.J. (1979) Conviction records of fathers and sons compared. *British Journal of Criminology*. 19, 120–133.

Oxford, T. (1991) Spotting a liar. *Police Review*, 328–329.

Palmer, E.J. & Hollin, C.R. (2000) The interrelations of socio-moral reasoning, perceptions on parenting and attributions of intent with self-reported delinquency. *Legal and Criminological Psychology*, 5, 201–218.

Pearse, J. & Gudjonsson, G. (1996) Police interviewing techniques in two south London police stations. *Psychology, Crime and Law*. 3, 63–74.

Pease, K. (1994) Crime Prevention, in M.Maguire, R. Morgan & R. Reiner (eds) *Oxford Handbook of Criminology*. Oxford: Oxford University Press.

Pease, K. (1998) *Repeat Victimisation: Taking stock*. Crime Prevention and Detection Series Paper 90. London: Home Office Police Research Group.

Pennington, N. & Hastie, R. (1990) Practical implications of psychological research on juror and jury decision-making. *Personality and Social Psychology Bulletin*. 16 (1), 90–105.

Peters, D. (1987) The impact of naturally occurring stress on children's memory. In Ceci, S.J., Toglia, M.P. & Ross, D.F. (eds) *Children's Eyewitness Memory*. New York: Springer-Verlag.

Perkins, D. (1990) Clinical treatment of sex offenders in secure settings. In C.R. Hollin & K. Howells (eds) *Clinical Approaches to Sex Offenders and their Victims*. Chichester: Wiley.

Pfeifer, J.E. & Ogloff, J.R. (1991) Ambiguity and guilt determinations: A modern racism perspective. *Journal of Applied Social Psychology*. 21 (21) 1713–1725.

Piaget, J. (1959) *Language and Thought of the Child*. London: Routledge and Kegan Paul.

Piliavin, I. & Briar, S. (1964) Police Encounters with Juveniles. *American Journal of Sociology*. 70 (2), 206–214.

Pithers, W.D. (1993) Treatment of rapists: Interpretation of early outcome data and exploratory constructs to enhance thereapeutic efficiency. In G.D. Nagayama Hall, R. Hirschman, J.R. Graham & M.S. Zaragoza (eds) *Sexual Aggression: Issues in Etiology, Assessment and Treatment*. Washington: Taylor and Francis.

Pinizzotto, A.J. & Finkel, N.J. (1990) Criminal personality profiling: An outcome and process study. *Law and Human Behaviour*. 14 (3), 215–233.

Plomin, R. (1994) *Genetics and Experience: The developmental interplay between nature and nurture*. Newbury Park: Sage.

Plomin, R. (2001) Genetics and Behaviour. *The Psychologist*. 14 (3), 134–139.

Pope, H.G., Oliva, P.S. & Hudson, J.J. (1999) The scientific status of research on repressed memories. In D.L. Faigman, D.H. Kaye, M.J. Saks & J.Sanders (eds) *Modern Scientific Evidence: The law and science of expert testimony*. St. Paul, MN: West Group.

Povey, D. & Prime, J. (1999) *Recorded Crime Statistics: England and Wales 1998–99*. Home Office Statistical Bulletin, 18/99. London: HMSO.

Povey, D., Cotton, J. & Sisson, S. (2001) *Recorded Crime Statistics: England and Wales 2000–2001*. Home Office Statistical Bulletin, 12/01. London: HMSO.

Prentky, R. (1995) A rational for the treatment of sex offenders: Pro bono publico. In J. McGuire (ed) *What works? Reducing offending*. Chichester: Wiley.

Price, W.H., Strong, J.A., Whatmore, P.B. & McClemont, W.F.(1966) Criminal patients with XYY sex-chromosome complement. *The Lancet*. 1, 565–566.

Quinsey, V.L, Harris, G.T., Rice, M.E. & Cormier, C.A. (1998) *Violent offenders:*

Appraising and managing risk. Washington DC: American Psychological Association.

Raine, A. (1993) *The Psychopathology of Crime: Criminal behaviour as a criminal disorder.* San Diego, CA: Academic Press.

Read, T. & Tilley, N. (2000) *Not rocket science? Problem-solving and crime reduction*. Crime Reduction Research Series, Paper 6. London: HMSO.

Reese, J.T. (1995) A history of police psychological services. In M.I. Kirke & E.M. Scrivner (eds) *Police Psychology into the 21st Century*. Hillsdale: Lawrence Erlbaum.

Reiner, R. (1997) Policing and the Police. In M. Maguire, R. Morgan & R. Reiner (eds) *The Oxford Handbook of Criminology*. Oxford: Oxford University Press.

Reiner, R. (1993) Race, Crime and Justice: Models of interpretation. In L.Gelsthorpe & W. McWilliam (eds) *Minority Ethnic Groups and the Criminal Justice System*. Cambridge: Cambridge University Institute of Criminology.

Resnick, H.S., Kilpatrick, D.G., Dansky, B.S., Saunders, B.E. & Best, C.L. (1993) Prevalence of civilian trauma and post-traumatic stress disorder in a representative national sample of women. *Journal of Consulting and Clinical Psychology.* 61, 984–991.

Ressler, R.K, Burgess, A.W. & Douglas, J.E. (1988) *Sexual Homicide: Patterns and Motives*. Lexington: Lexington Books.

Ressler, R.K., Douglas, J.E., Burgess, A.W. & Burgess, A.G. (1992) *The Crime Classification Manual*. New York: Simon and Schuster.

Ross, L. (1977) The intuitive psychologist and his shortcomings: Distortions in the attribution process. In L. Berkowitz (ed) *Advances in Experimental Social Psychology*. New York: Academic Press.

Ross, R.R., Fabiano, E.A. & Ewles, C.D. (1988) Reasoning and rehabilitation. *International Journal of Offender Therapy and Comparative Criminology.* 20, 29–35.

Ross, D.F., Hopkins, S., Hanson, E., Lindsay, R.C.L., Hazen, K. & Eslinger, T. (1994) The impact of protective shields and videotape testimony on conviction rates in a simulated trial of child sexual abuse. *Law and Human Behavior.* 18, 553–566.

Rossmo, D.K. (1996) Targeting victims: Serial killers and the urban environment. In T. O'Reilly-Fleming (ed) *Serial and Mass Murder: Theory, research and policy*. Toronto: Canadian Scholars Press.

Rossmo, D.K. (1997) Geographic Profiling. In J.L. Jackson & D.A. Bekarian (eds) *Offender Profiling: Theory, Research and Practice.* Chichester: Wiley.

Rosenhan, D.L. (1973) On being sane in insane places. *Science.* 179, 250–258.

Rotter, J.B. (1966) Generalized expectancies for internal versus external control of reinforcement. *Psychological Monographs.* 80 (609).

Rotter, J.B. (1975) Some problems and misconceptions related to the construct of internal versus external control of reinforcement. *Journal of Consulting and Clinical Psychology*. 43, 56–67.

Rowe, D.G. (1990) Inherited dispositions towards learning delinquent and criminal behaviour: New evidence. In L. Ellis & H. Hoffman (eds) *Crime in Biological, Social and Moral Contexts*. New York: Praeger.

Rushton, J.P. (1990) Race and crime: A reply to Roberts and Gabor. *Canadian Journal of Criminology*. 32, 315–334.

Rutter, M. (1971) *Maternal Deprivation Re-assessed*. Harmondsworth: Penguin.

Sandys, M. & Dillehay, R.C. (1995) First-ballot votes, predeliberation dispositions and final verdicts in jury trials. *Law and Human Behaviour*. 19, 175–195.

Seltzer, R., Venuti, M.A. & Lopes, G.M. (1991) Juror honesty during *voir dire*. *Journal of Criminal Justice*. 19 (5), 451–462.

Shaw, C. & McKay, H. (1942) *Juvenile Delinquency and Urban Areas*. Chicago: University of Chicago Press.

Shaw, M. (1999) A bereavement model of the emotional scars of chronic victimisation. In Farrell, G. & Pease, K. (eds) *Repeat Victimization*. New York: Criminal Justice Press.

Sheldon, W.H. (1942) *The Varieties of Temperament: A psychology of constitutional differences.* New York: Harper.

Shepherd, J.W., Davies, G.M., & Ellis, H.D. (1978) How best shall a face be described? In P.M. Morris & R.N. Sykes (eds) *Practical Aspects of Memory*. London: Academic Press.

Sigall, H. & Ostrove, N. (1975) Beautiful but dangerous: Effects of offender attractiveness and nature of crime on juridic judgement. *Journal of Personality and Social Psychology.* 31, 401–414.

Siegal, L.J. (1986) *Criminology*. St Paul, MN: West Publishing.

Smart, C. (1977) *Women, Crime and Criminology*. London: Routledge.

Smart, C. (1990) Feminist approaches to criminology or postmodern woman meets atavistic man. In L. Gelsthorpe & A. Morris (eds) *Feminist Perspectives in Criminology*. Buckingham: Open University Press.

Smolowe, J. (1995) TV cameras on trial: The unseemly Simpson spectacle provokes a backlash against televised proceedings. *Time*, 24th July.

Steller, M. & Kohnken, G. (1989) Criteria based statement analysis. In D.C. Raskin (ed) *Psychological Methods in Criminal Investigation and Evidence*. New York: Springer-Verlag.

Stephenson, G.M. (1992) *The Psychology of Criminal Justice*. Oxford: Blackwell.

Stewart, J.E. (1980) Defendant's attractiveness as a factor in the outcome of criminal trials: An observational study. *Journal of Applied Social Psychology*. 10, 348–361.

Stoner, J.A.F. (1968) Risky and cautious shifts in group decisions: the influence of widely held values. *Journal of Experimental Social Psychology*. 4, 442–459.

Strodtbeck, F.I., James, J. & Hawkins, C. (1957) Social status in jury deliberations. *American Sociological Review*. 22, 713–719.

Sutherland, E.H. (1939) *Principles of Criminology*. Philadelphia: Lippincott.

Thomson, D.M. (1995) Eyewitness testimony and identification tests. In N. Brewer & C. Wilson (eds) *Psychology and Policing*. Hillsdale, NJ: Lawrence Erlbaum.

Thornton, D.M. (1987) Treatment effects on recidivism: A reappraisal of the 'nothing works' doctrine. In B.J. McGurk, D.M. Thornton & M. Williams (eds) *Applying Psychology to Imprisonment: Theory and practice*. London: HMSO.

Tomsen, S. (1997) A top night – social protest, masculinity and the culture of drinking violence. *British Journal of Criminology*. 37 (1), 90–102.

Towl, G.J. & Crighton, D. (1996) *Handbook of Psychology for Forensic Practitioners*. London: Sage.

Trasler, G.B. (1978) Relations between psychopathy and persistent criminality. In R.D. Hare & D. Schalling (eds) *Psychopathic Behavior: Approaches to research*. New York: John Wiley.

Trasler, G.B. (1987) Biogenetic Factors. In H.C. Quay (ed) *Handbook of Juvenile Delinquency*. New York: John Wiley.

Utting, G. (1996) *Reducing criminality among young people: A sample of relevant programmes in the United Kingdom*. Home Office Research Study No. 161. London: HMSO.

Van den Haag, E. (1982) Could successful rehabilitation reduce the crime rate? *Journal of Criminal Law and Criminology*. 73, 1022–1035.

Vold, G.B., Bernard, T.J. & Snipes, J.B. (1998) *Theoretical Criminology*. Oxford: Oxford University Press.

Vrij, A. (1998) Nonverbal communication and credibility. In A. Memon, A. Vrij, & R. Bull (eds) *Psychology and Law: Truthfulness, accuracy and credibility*. Maidenhead: McGraw-Hill.

Vrij, A. & Parker, I. (1997) Sensationalism and number of reports as indicators of fear of crime: An experiment with broadsheet and tabloid newspapers. In G.M. Stephenson & N. Clark (eds) *Procedures of Criminal Justice: Contemporary psychological issues*. Issues in Criminological and Legal Psychology, no. 29. London: British Psychological Society.

Walklate, S. (2001) *Gender, Crime and Criminal Justice*. Cullompton: Willan Publishing.

Wallbott, H.G. (1996) Social Psychology and the Media. In G.R. Semin & K. Fiedler (eds) *Applied Social Psychology*. London: Sage.

Walters, G.D. (1992) A meta-analysis of the gene–crime relationship. *Criminology*. 30, 595–613.

Wells, G.L., Small, M., Penrod, S., Malpass, R., Fulero, S.M. & Brimacombe,

C.A.E. (1998) Eyewitness identification procedures: Recommendations for line-ups and photospreads. *Law and Human Behaviour*. 23 (6), 603–647.

Westcott, H., Davies, G. & Bull, R. (2001) *Children's Testimony*. Chichester: Wiley.

White, E.K. & Honig, A.L. (1995) The role of the police psychologist in training. In M.I. Kurke & E.M. Scrivner (eds) *Police Psychology into the 21st Century*. Hillsdale, NJ: Lawrence Erlbaum.

Wilbanks, W. (1987) *The Myth of a Racist Criminal Justice System*. Monterey: Brooks/Cole.

Williamson, T.M. (1990) Strategic changes in police interrogation. Unpublished PhD thesis, University of Kent. Cited in Ainsworth, P.B. (2000) *Psychology and Crime: Myths and reality*. Harlow: Pearson

Wilson, J.Q. & Kelling, G. (1982) Broken windows. *The Atlantic Monthly*, March, 29–38.

Wilson, J.Q. & Herrnstein, R.J. (1985) *Crime and Human Nature*. New York: Touchstone.

Witkin, H.A., Mednick, S.A., Schulsinger, F., Bakkestrom, E., Christiansen, K.O., Goodenough, D.R., Hirschorn, K., Lundsteen, C., Owen, D.R., Philip, J., Rubin, D.B. & Stocking, M.M. (1976) Criminality in XYY and XXY men. *Science*. 193, 547–555.

Wright, D.B. & McDaid, A.T. (1996) Comparing system and estimator variables using data from real line-ups. *Applied Cognitive Psychology*. 10, 75–84.

Wulach, J. (1988) The criminal personality as a DSM-III-R antisocial, narcissistic, borderline, and histrionic personality disorder. *International Journal of Offender Therapy and Comparative Criminology*. 32, 185–199.

Yarmey, A.D. (1992) Accuracy of eyewitness and earwitness show-up identification in a field setting. Poster presented at the *American Psychology-Law Society Conference*. San Diego, California.

Yates, E., Barbaree, H.E. & Marshall, W.L. (1984) Anger and deviant arousal. *Behavior Therapy*. 15, 287–294.

Yochelson, S. & Samenow, S.E. (1976) *The Criminal Personality, Volume 1: A profile for change*. New York: Jason Aronsen.

Yuille, J.C. & Cutshall, J.L. (1986) A case study of eyewitness memory of a crime. *Journal of Applied Psychology*. 71, 291–301.

Zigler, E. & Hall, N.W. (1987) The implications of early intervention for the primary prevention of juvenile delinquence. In J.Q. Wilson & G.C. Loury (eds) *From Children to Citizens: Volume 3: Families, Schools and Delinquency Prevention*. New York: Springer-Verlag.

Zimbardo, P.G., Banks, W.C., Craig, H. & Jaffe, D. (1973) A Pirandellian Prison: The mind is a formidable jailor. *New York Times Magazine*, April 8, 38–60.

Index